WITHDRAWN

DATE DUE

MAY 4 1992	
MAY 2 0 1992	
APR 1 6 1994	
MAY 1 5 1995	

Human Rights and the
Conflict of Cultures

Studies in Comparative Religion
Frederick M. Denny, *Editor*

The Holy Book in Comparative Perspective
Edited by Frederick M. Denny and Rodney L. Taylor

Dr. Strangegod: On the Symbolic Meaning of Nuclear Weapons
By Ira Chernus

Native American Religious Action: A Performance Approach to Religion
by Sam Gill

The Confucian Way of Contemplation
by Rodney Taylor

Human Rights and the Conflict of Cultures:

Western and Islamic Perspectives on Religious Liberty

BY David Little, John Kelsay, and Abdulaziz A. Sachedina

University of
South Carolina Press

Published in Columbia, South Carolina, by the
University of South Carolina Press

Excerpts from *The Koran Interpreted,* translated by A. J. Arberry, Allen & Unwin, Inc.,
1980, are reprinted with the permission of the publisher.

LIBRARY OF CONGRESS
Library of Congress Cataloging-in-Publication Data

Little, David.
    Human rights and the conflict of cultures : Western and Islamic
    perspectives on religious liberty / by David Little, John Kelsay,
    and Abdulaziz A. Sachedina.
       p.   cm.—(Studies in comparative religion)
    Bibliography: p.
    Includes index.
    ISBN 0–87249–533–7
     1. Human rights—Religious aspects—Comparative studies. 2. Human
rights—Religious aspects—Christianity. 3. Human rights—Religious
aspects—Islam. I. Kelsay, John, 1953– . II. Sachedina,
Abdulaziz Abdulhussein, 1942– . III. Title.   IV. Series: Studies
in comparative religion (Columbia, S.C.)
    BL65.H78L57 1988
    291.1'772—dc19   88–7291
                                                       CIP

To All Those Who Have
Stood for the
Inalienable Rights
of Humanity

Contents

Editor's Preface

This volume in the series Studies in Comparative Religion is probably rather different from what most readers would expect in a field where the focus is usually on such topics as myth, ritual, sacred time and space, holy communities, religious leadership roles, scripture, and other customary phenomena. However, we view comparative religion as embracing a broad range of related scholars and disciplines united by a desire to understand religions and theoretical and methodological issues in the study of religion from a global perspective. In this case the focus is on an issue in comparative religious ethics that has received little scholarly attention to date.

Human Rights and the Conflict of Cultures: Western and Islamic Perspectives on Religious Liberty is evidence that the relatively new field of comparative religious ethics is increasing both in power and scope. David Little is one of the formative thinkers in this field and his writings—mostly treating Christian or otherwise Western ethical and sociological subjects—have greatly influenced its development. Abdulaziz A. Sachedina is a distinguished Shi'ite scholar whose education both in Muslim institutions and the West has made him one of a small company of specialists capable of providing authentic analyses and interpretations bridging East and West. He works from a profound knowledge of Islamic life and thought, but he is equally sensitive to the feelings and ways of understanding of people outside his tradition. John Kelsay was trained in comparative religious ethics and Islamic studies by Little and Sachedina and is therefore one of the first people to be launched in his career with a deliberate combination of the two fields. This book is thus very much a pioneering venture that was conceived and nurtured within the daily academic give and take of a graduate student and his two advisers at the University of Virginia.

The authors have worked closely with each other at every stage of this volume's preparation thus ensuring a high degree of unity of vision and coherence of objectives. This is not to suggest that they necessarily agree on every point. The notion of a right to freedom of religion and conscience will be viewed by some as an essentially Western and modern issue that has questionable application to Islam, which has its own deep and abiding convictions about the human condition and its ultimate destiny. Yet freedom of religion and conscience does have a global relevance, especially since the drawing up of the Universal Declaration of Human Rights after World War II. That document and other sources of Christian and otherwise Western origin, as well as Islamic texts, most notably the Qur'an, provide the fundamental data for this study.

Human Rights and the Conflict of Cultures is not the last word on what is a vast and complex subject; it is, rather, a thoughtful exercise in "intercultural dialogue," as the authors characterize their enterprise. Such a dialogue is intellectually well grounded in the approach of this study, which wisely pairs Islam with the West, rather than with the whole of Christianity. There are very many Westerners who are not religious, but who nevertheless adhere to a belief in freedom of religion and conscience; whereas Muslims, wherever they reside, usually have a shared view concerning the subject. Christianity is but one major source in the West's convictions about freedom of religion and conscience. For Muslims, their religious teachings on the issue are fundamental, regardless of culture. But as this study shows, a Muslim approach to the subject can be both traditionally based and intellectually creative and open.

Frederick M. Denny
General Editor
Studies in Comparative Religion

Human Rights and the
Conflict of Cultures

Introduction

This book, as its title suggests, is concerned with the possibilities and problems of claims about (as well as to or for) "human rights" in a culturally diverse world. In particular, the authors are concerned with the relationship between religion and human rights—with the ways that certain religious traditions may or may not provide support for ideas expressed in various international documents, especially ideas of religious liberty or freedom of conscience. The book is not concerned, then, with the question of the philosophical status of human rights claims. Nor is it concerned with the variety of legal questions that arise in connection with the implication that there is, or might be, a recognized standard of behavior with international validity, accompanied by sanctions administered by an international authority. It is rather an essay or a set of essays in comparative religious ethics framed according to the issue of human rights. The organization or strategy of these essays and the larger aims they are intended to serve are outlined in what follows.

The Strategy of This Study

Pollis and Schwab conclude their essay "Human Rights: A Western Construct with Limited Applicability" by expressing a familiar objection to ethnocentrism: "Unfortunately not only do human rights set forth in the Universal Declaration reveal a strong western bias, but there has been a tendency to view human rights ahistorically and in isolation from their social, political and economic milieu."[1]

3

This criticism is frequently applied to statements of rights concerning private property, vacations with pay, the status of women, marriage arrangements, forms of punishment, and some particular political and civil guarantees, such as voting procedures, that are contained in various "internationally recognized" human rights documents. The complaint is that these are so many manifestations of a highly parochial cultural and historical experience that, at certain points, neither does have nor ought to have anything definitive to say to peoples with other experience and traditions.

The charge is a serious and challenging one. Human rights advocates need to face it squarely and respond to it with precision and care. Are all the rights contained in the documents equally binding upon all peoples everywhere? Or are some rights (more than others) subject to national and cultural discretion? Which ones? And how much discretion? Ought it simply be up to each government and each culture to pick and choose among the catalogs of rights and decide which ones are binding and which ones not? Or are at least some rights indefeasible and absolute whatever particular governments and societies, in accord with their cultural traditions, may decide? In short, are human rights—all, or in part—the measure of governments and cultures, or are governments and cultures the measure of human rights?

These are staggeringly large questions. They go to the heart of political, legal, and moral theory, including the study of comparative ethics. We do not begin to have a comprehensive answer, and we doubt that such an answer is even possible at this rather primitive stage of reflection on human rights questions. But it is necessary to make some preliminary attempts. We propose to do that by considerably narrowing the range of inquiry, and by taking up particular charges of Western bias and cultural discrimination that have persistently been lodged by Muslims and by Western students of Islam against the statements in various human rights documents concerning the right to freedom of thought, conscience, and religion. By examining and evaluating in detail the disagreements between Islamic culture and proponents of the Western tradition over just one of the alleged human rights—the right to freedom of conscience and religion—we may begin to see how we might go at the bigger problems.

Many of the Muslim objections were first registered in 1948 during the deliberations that surrounded Article 18 of the Universal Declaration, which states: "Everyone has the right to freedom of thought, conscience and religion; this right includes freedom to change his religion or belief, and freedom, either alone or in community with others in public or in private, to manifest his religion or belief in teaching, practice, worship and observance."[2] In response, a number of Islamic countries (in particular, Saudi

Arabia) attempted to delete this article. Failing that, they blamed others—Lebanon, for example—for supporting it because, they contended, the rights of Lebanese Muslims would be compromised by such wording.

Objections were raised by some of the same countries against the somewhat more elaborate version of the right to religious freedom contained in the draft of the International Covenant on Civil and Political Rights, which was later adopted and which stated: "No one shall be subject to coercion which would impair his freedom to have or to adopt a religion or belief of his choice" (Article 18, sect. 2). And Article 26 of the Covenant added another new stipulation which guaranteed equal protection of the law against any form of discrimination "on any ground such as race, . . . sex, . . . [or] religion."[3]

More recently, objections from much the same quarter were again raised in reaction to the draft of the Declaration on the Elimination of All Forms of Intolerance and of Discrimination Based on Religion or Belief. The dissenting views that were advanced in the discussions of the Human Rights Commission actually had some limited effect on the final version of the Declaration. In that version, which the United Nations General Assembly adopted on 25 November, 1981, some of the wording that referred to a right to choose, adopt, or change one's religion was deleted, although by no means uniformly. In any case, in Article 8 of the Declaration, the General Assembly made clear it considered the earlier statements of the right to choose and change one's own religion contained in the Universal Declaration and the Covenant on Political and Civil Rights to be fully binding.[4] Furthermore, Article 2 of the Declaration adds some new stipulations of its own.

1. No one shall be subject to discrimination by any State, institution, group of persons or person on grounds of religion or other belief.
2. For the purposes of the present Declaration, the expression "intolerance and discrimination based on religion or belief" means any distinction, exclusion, restriction or preference based on religion or belief and having as its purpose or as its effect nullification or impairment of the recognition, enjoyment or exercise of human rights and fundamental freedoms on an equal basis.

The reactions of Muslim political officials and religious leaders to the idea that human beings have a basic right to follow their consciences, change religion as they see fit, and be free of discriminatory treatment based on religious belief are, for the most part, well summarized as follows:

A major area of disagreement is freedom of religion. The Qur'an vigorously denounces those who renounce Islam, for "the Devil has seduced them" away from the true faith (67:25). The major historical example is the revolt of the tribes after Muhammad's death in A.D. 632. Abu Bakr, and jurists since then, condemned secession from Islam (*ridda*) as doubly heinous: It not only is a violation of the compact of submission made with Allah, but it is also a breach of contract with his representatives on earth. It is, then, an offense both against God and against the state: it is both apostasy and treason. Far from having the right to become non-Muslim, the Muslim faces the death penalty as a sanction for such a charge.[5]

The message of the Qur'an is preoccupied with what might be called the political threat of religious unbelief. Muhammad's campaign to solidify and extend his political authority depended on religious as well as political loyalty from the contending factions. His struggle to subdue Medina and Mecca by creating an intricate confederation was wrought out of severe and constant struggles against these religio-political factions, and stability was constantly threatened by one or another of them.

These facts help explain the intensity of some Qur'anic utterances concerning apostasy and the reasons for recommending the use of force in some cases against apostates.[6]

They [the disbelievers] wish that you should disbelieve as
they disbelieve, and then you would be
equal; therefore take not yourselves
friends of them, until they emigrate in
the way of God; then, if they turn their backs,
take them, and slay them wherever you find them;
take not to yourselves any one of them as friend or helper. (4:89)

This is the recompense of those who fight
against God and His Messenger, and hasten
about the earth, to do corruption there:
they shall be slaughtered, or crucified, or their hands and feet shall
   alternately
be struck off, or they shall be banished
from the land. That is a degradation for them
in this world; and in the world to come awaits them a mighty
   chastisement. (5:33)

Fight those who believe not in God and the Last Day
and do not forbid what God and His Messenger
have forbidden—such men as practise not the

religion of truth, being of those who have been given
the Book—until they pay the tribute out of hand and have been humbled.
  (9:29)

These passages are supplemented by certain statements of Muhammad, as reported in the *hadith* (sayings of Muhammad or narratives concerning him): "He who changes his religion must be killed," and by other reports from the same source that apostates were occasionally punished by losing hands and feet before being killed. Accordingly, apostasy has come to be included in Islamic law as one of the *hudad,* or capital crimes, along with adultery, defamation and slander, alcoholism, theft, brigandage, treason, and armed rebellion. The conflict at this point between conventional Islamic interpretation and the prescriptions of the human rights documents concerning a right not to be subject to "coercion which would impair [one's] freedom to have or adopt a religion or belief of his choice" would appear to be acute.

There is also the question, in the words of sections 1 and 2 of Article 2 of the Declaration against Intolerance, concerning legal discrimination "on grounds of religion and other belief"—that is, of "any distinction, exclusion, restriction or preference based on religion or belief." Even though, as is well known, non-Muslim monotheists (*dhimmis*) namely Jews, Christians, Zoroastrians, and some others—are traditionally treated more tolerantly than polytheists and other kinds of "disbelievers," they are hardly accorded full and equal rights. So long as they live peaceably, they may practice their religion (in a subdued manner); but they are nevertheless required to pay a tax (*jizya*) to the Islamic state—described by one scholar "as a form of punishment of unbelief."[7]

What is more, Muslim authorities may prohibit the *dhimmis* from marrying Muslims and from conducting certain forms of business, and the *dhimmis* may be required, according to traditional Islamic law, to wear distinctive clothing and to live in houses smaller than Muslim houses. Finally, in certain Islamic states non-Muslims are prevented from occupying high public office, as, for example, in Pakistan and most Arab states, where the head of state must be a Muslim. In short, the record shows that non-Muslims in Muslim countries do not enjoy the rights to life and liberty in the same measure as the Muslims. Or as Majid Khadduri puts it, "As a subject of the Muslim state [*the dhimmi*] suffered certain disabilities which reduced him to the status of a second-class citizen."[8]

The conflict, then, seems clear. The articles on freedom of religion and conscience in various human rights documents appear to run afoul, at important points, of much established and official Muslim teaching about the treatment of apostates and protected non-Muslims. There are at least four possible strategies we might adopt in face of this conflict:

1. We might simply advocate retracting all statements in favor of freedom of religion and conscience (or we might accomplish the same purpose by rewriting existing statements so as to make them innocuous). There are problems with this response. Are all human rights statements to be retracted or emasculated whenever they encounter opposition? But, more to the point, there is actually little interest in the international community, even among Muslims, in taking such a radical step. Muslims, like others, seem committed to giving human rights status to freedom of religion and conscience, so long as those rights are properly restricted according to traditional teaching.

2. We might try to argue that devotion to existing freedom of religion statements entails allowing Muslim states, along with everyone else, discretion to define religious tolerance and its limits in whatever way they see fit. We would then be allowing Muslims the right to follow their own consciences, and thus act on their internationally guaranteed right to religious liberty. There are two problems here. One is that tolerating all views, even the most intolerant ones, yields a contradictory policy, especially when intolerance toward certain beliefs can be enforced. Equally troublesome is the fact that existing statements of the right to religious liberty explicitly include prohibitions that contradict certain Muslim policies.

3. We might cling to existing statements of the right to religious liberty and attempt to enforce them internationally by means of the same devices that the United States, for example, has from time to time employed in trying to enforce other civil, political, and economic rights. There are no doubt special problems of feasibility in this case. Moreover, without agreeing that a belief in freedom of religion entails tolerating any belief, even those that enforce intolerance, it does seem that the cultural differences over this question create some subtleties and perplexities for human rights advocates that are not present in respect to the more notorious violations, such as gross mistreatment of prisoners, political opponents, etc.

4. We might use the contemporary debate between Westerners and Muslims over freedom of religion and conscience as an occasion for reconsidering the foundations and character of a belief in such freedom both in the West and in the Islamic tradition. If, upon careful, critical examination, the conflict between Western and Islamic views concerning something so important and so basic as a right to freedom of religion and conscience turns out to be much less clear and consistent than has been alleged, then we shall, it seems, have some reason to begin to call into question the "limited applicability" of human rights declarations.

In this volume we adopt the fourth strategy. We are convinced that the subject of human rights in general and the right to freedom of religion and conscience in particular has suffered in the West from a fashionable but unconvincing belief in relativism, and in the Islamic world from a failure to subject the Qur'anic foundations of Islamic faith to rigorous and sympathetic reexamination, as well as failure to acknowledge the internal complexity of the Islamic tradition in regard to those matters.

Our attempt is couched, to some degree, in the form of an intercultural dialogue. David Little, while concerned with and committed to the cross-cultural comparison of religio-ethical systems, approaches these questions out of a Western background and primarily Western training. His role in this project is conceived on the model of certain early-twentieth-century students of society and religion such as Max Weber and Ernst Troeltsch.[9] Although lacking technical competence in non-Western traditions, Weber and Troeltsch saw fit to suggest frameworks of analysis for the comparative examination of Western and non-Western religions and patterns of social behavior. They used their proposed frameworks to generate "plausible hypotheses" that required careful scrutiny and correction by experts in the respective traditions. Their suggestions were, in short, viewed as invitations to intercultural discussion and mutual reflection. Little's proposals for identifying salient parallels between Western and Islamic beliefs about freedom of religion and conscience in chapter 1 are submitted in that spirit.

Abdulaziz Sachedina's discussion in chapter 3 supplies the sort of expert and critical response to Little's hypothesis that the Weber-Troeltsch approach calls for. Although partially trained in the West, Sachedina comes out of a Muslim background and is schooled in the languages and scholarship of Islam. His arguments concerning the Qur'anic basis for a fairly radical doctrine of religious freedom are no doubt controversial. However, judging from the preliminary reaction to his views by some Muslims and Islamic scholars, his interpretation will command serious consideration from those qualified to judge.

John Kelsay represents something of a "bridge figure" in this endeavor. He is a recent product of the graduate program in religious ethics at the University of Virginia, and, like Little, his primary training and background are in Western Christianity. Still, working closely with Sachedina, he has begun to develop special competence in Islam by learning Arabic and studying the history and thought of Islam. His discussion in chapter 2, of the diversity within Islam concerning views toward freedom of religion and conscience as registered in some of the United Nations debates over international human rights instruments seeks to substantiate the existence within Islam itself of a diversity of opinion concerning questions of religious liberty, which challenges the accuracy of a number of Western portrayals of that tradition.

Whether the ideas expressed in this volume finally stand up or not, all three authors wish to encourage others to undertake a similarly "dialogic" approach to intercultural study. Their firm conviction is that complicated subjects like this one are too big for any one person and require cooperation among individuals with diverse backgrounds and competences such as the different authors bring to this study.

Larger Objectives

While this project is—for good reason, we believe—rather sharply focused on the problem of whether there exists across cultures a human right to freedom of religion and conscience, there remain some larger background considerations having to do with the comparative study of religious ethics that we want to address in a preliminary way during the course of our argument.

In recent years considerable debate has raged over the sheer possibility of crosscultural and crossreligious comparisons. The doubts of Pollis and Schwab about the universal applicability of human rights categories, quoted earlier, are simply expanded into general doubts about the applicability of any encompassing categories like "religion" or "morality" to diverse traditions.[10]

For example, phrases like "the world's religions"—when used to suggest that the world's sacred traditions all share common and comparable characteristics—have been sharply challenged by scholars such as Wilfred Cantwell Smith. In *The Meaning and End of Religion* Smith argues that the notion "religion" is itself the product of the special and rather jaundiced experience of the West.[11] With the growth, after the Enlightenment, of secularism and the scientific and comparative study of sacred traditions, the word "religion" became an outsider's way of describing those traditions. Rather than capturing what, at bottom, it meant to people from their own perspective to be Christians or Muslims or Buddhists or Jews, the beliefs, institutions, and practices of these people were coldly and abstractly arranged and classified for them, and then common elements among the world's religions were "objectively" identified by "expert spectators." So understood, the whole idea of comparative religion missed the point of the crucial experience of these people, which is, for Smith, "something deep, personal and transcendentally oriented." As used, the term "religion" became perjorative, either in the service of reductionistic inquiry by scientists of religion or as a way of individiously misdescribing sacred traditions other than one's own.

The problem here is that Smith's recommendation about excising the word "religion" from comparative discussions of sacred traditions is itself ambiguous. He advocates dropping the notion in all but the "personalistic" sense, as he says—namely, the sense of deep inward piety or heartfelt personal commitment to something transcendent. But that means that Smith has not, on his own account, dispensed with the idea of religion as a bridge term for comparative study. He simply has specified the term in his own way, and then urged comparing the world's sacred traditions according to what *he* regards as the essential religious element. Smith may be right or wrong in doing that, but in any case he has not, even by his own lights, made it impossible any longer to endeavor meaningfully to compare the world's religions.

While we cannot hope in this limited study to provide a comprehensive defense of the intercultural applicability of the notion of religion—or, for that matter, of human rights—we shall endeavor to work our way some distance in that direction. We shall do that by trying to show that it makes considerable sense to compare examples of "the world's religions" like Western Christianity and Islam around the subject of freedom of religion and conscience.

NOTES

1. Adamantia Pollis and Peter Schwab, *Human Rights: Cultural and Ideological Perspectives* (New York: Praeger, 1979), 17.

2. *Human Rights Documents*, 98th Cong. 1st sess., 1983, Committee Print, 66.

3. *Human Rights Documents*, 85.

4. General Assembly Resolution 55, 25 Nov. 1982, General Assembly Official Record, supp. 48, A/36/48/1981. See Appendix. Cf. Sidney Liskofsky. "The UN Declaration on the Elimination of Religious Intolerance and Discrimination: Historical and Legal Perspectives," *Religion and the State*, ed. James E. Wood, Jr. (Waco, Tex.: Baylor University Press, 1985), 441–83.

5. James P. Piscatori, "Human Rights in Islamic Political Culture," *The Moral Imperative of Human Rights*, ed. Kenneth W. Thompson (Washington: University Press of America, 1980), 145.

6. Unless otherwise noted, Qur'anic citations are from A. J. Arberry, *The Koran Interpreted* (New York: Macmillan, 1955).

7. Majid Khadduri, *War and Peace in the Law of Islam* (Baltimore: Johns Hopkins Press, 1955), 198.

8. Khadduri, *War and Peace*, 196.

9. Max Weber's elaborate attempts to compare the world's religions in respect to fundamental "ideal" and "material" interests of human beings are best summarized in the section called

Human Rights and the Conflict of Cultures

"Sociology of Religion" in *Economy and Society* (Totawa, N.J.: Bedminster Press, 1968). Ernst Troeltsch's efforts in this regard are best represented in his *The Absoluteness of Christianity and the History of Religions* (Richmond: John Knox Press, 1971) and *Christian Thought: Its History and Application* (New York: Meridian Books, 1957). The Troeltschian background of the approach adopted in this volume is extensively discussed in an unpublished paper by Little, "Human Rights and the World's Religions," from which some of the discussion in the first chapter is drawn.

10. See the debates in Bryan Wilson, ed., *Rationality* (Oxford: Blackwell, 1970); Martin Hollis and Steven Lukes, eds., *Rationality and Relativism* (Cambridge: MIT Press, 1982); Michael Krausz and Jack W. Meiland, eds., *Relativism: Cognitive and Moral* (Notre Dame: University of Notre Dame Press, 1982); see also Steven Lukes, "Relativism: Cognitive and Moral," *Aristotelian Society Supplementary* 48 (1974): 165–89. Cf. David Little and Sumner Twiss, *Comparative Religious Ethics* (New York: Harper, 1978).

11. Wilfred Cantwell Smith, *The Meaning and End of Religion* (New York: New American library, 1964), 42.

Part I: The Development in the West of the Right to Freedom of Religion and Conscience: A Basis for Comparison with Islam

1. The Western Tradition.

That the history of Western Christianity is really one long and many-sided controversy over the proper interpretation of freedom of religion and conscience is not surprising given the condition and character of the early Christian church. Deliberately to call believers out from the world (the Greek word for church means "called out") and thereby to set those believers apart from civil power, as well as from the determinants of kin, station, and ethnic identity, is to intensify personal self-awareness and the sense of personal responsibility for spiritual self-direction and affiliation.

In particular, by restricting the legitimate control of civil coercion over religious life, the distinction between "personal" and "external" or "inner" and "outer" was heightened. To hold that true belief is not a matter of external causes, but of deeply felt inward motions, is to affirm, by implication, the importance of establishing a "free zone" where individuals are permitted to negotiate their spiritual life according to the dictates of their own best inner judgment.

It was no doubt because of this intensifying of inner, personal experience in early Christianity that the idea of conscience so soon became a natural and abiding focus of attention. It is worth noting, for example, the close etymological affiliation between "conscience" and "consciousness." The moral and religious significance that the term "conscience" has come to have presupposes the notion of self-knowledge or self-awareness—literally, "to know with oneself." As the idea of conscience developed in pre-Christian Hellenistic literature, it was conceived of as a private monitor, as a deeply internal, self-reflective, and self-critical operation that defined, at bottom, what it meant to be a self or a person. The conscience reviews "the quality of a man's own acts, and, it follows, of his own character. . . . [It] is not concerned with the acts, attitudes or characters of others. . . . The knowledge or awareness that a man has, the witness that he is in a position to bear—*is internal. No external authority need be consulted: he knows, and is his own witness to himself; and his knowledge and witness are private to him alone.'*"[1] Implicit in this view, of course, is the idea that human beings have implanted in them "by nature" a set of general requirements and standards of behavior, both formal and substantive, according to which the internal appraisal of one's own acts and character is conducted.

In addition, the conscience refers to specific acts; it is practical in being preoccupied with the circumstantial details of action, and the regnant image is judicial. The reference is always to reviewing *past* acts in order to determine guilt or innocence.[2] The judicial image extends to the function of sentencing for culpable misdeeds, and the punishment is, of course, the "pangs" of conscience.

These characteristics underlie Paul's appropriation of the concept in his epistles, as they underlie the entire Western tradition. But, as Eric d'Arcy points out, Paul innovated in two crucial respects.[3] In his discussion in 1 Corinthians of the pros and cons of eating meat offered to idols, Paul suggests, first, that the conscience is not exclusively judicial; it does not operate only retrospectively. In addition, it is "legislative" (or deliberative), which means that it also operates before the fact. One now is understood to struggle with one's conscience in anticipation of future action. Second, conscience is, as Paul's mention of a "doubtful, uneasy conscience" (1 Cor. 8:7) implies, taken to be subject to error. The condition of fallibility leads to the idea of erroneous conscience that was to become so important in the later development of religious liberty and freedom of conscience, as we shall see.

In addition, Paul reinforces and fills out somewhat the assumptions that were packed into the Roman and popular Greek notion of conscience. In Romans 2:14–15 he stresses the natural-moral grounds of conscience that are available to all human beings, Jew and Gentile alike. For example, in Romans 3:19 Paul emphasizes that these grounds are assumed to be objective and universal; according to them, "every mouth may be stopped, and the whole world may be held accountable to God." Finally, Paul draws attention to some of the particular requirements of what, out of the Western tradition, we have come to call "conscientiousness," namely the virtues of sincerity, veracity, and perseverance (e.g., see 2 Cor. 2:12ff).[4] And all this was given particular emphasis by institutionalizing these ideas in a separate community, in a social "context of conscience," so to speak, that was intentionally set apart from "the world."

There are two aspects of the history that need special emphasis. First, the struggle between conscience and the state—between the internal forum and the external forum, or between the sword of the spirit and the sword of steel, as the tension became described—was a persistent and painful struggle throughout Christian history, well before the seventeenth century and the first appearance of serious civil protection for religious liberty.

Much of significance in the development of the idea of conscience took place during the Middle Ages. The Catholic Scholastic disputes laid the groundwork for the influential analysis of conscience by Thomas Aquinas.[5] Two major features of Thomas's view are important: his description of conscience, and the kind and degree of freedom or sovereignty he believed it to have. As to its character, Thomas argued that conscience consists essentially of a rational act by which an individual undertakes to apply the first principles of the natural-moral law—what he called *synderesis* (borrowing from the Greeks)—to particular circumstances in which an individual is called upon to do or not do something. Thus, the conscience has a cognitive and logical feature: It assumes and draws upon indubitable first moral principles, and it has the capacity to identify and distinguish among objects and relations in the world according to commonly available canons of rationality. Moreover, since the conscience, so to speak, addresses and seeks to guide the will, it also has a conative feature. Finally, as the conscience in its judicial role can convince its owner of wrongdoing and cause remorse and the experience of guilt, it has an affective feature.[6]

Now it is important to note that Thomas intentionally provides us with at least the outlines of a normative model of the conscience. That is, if one's first principles are in order; if they are conscientiously, correctly, and consistently applied to the circumstances of a given case; and if the will, having heard the recommendation of the conscience, knowingly and deliberately— which is to say, freely—acts upon it; and, if the affections register favorably as they should; then this is an example of a righteous act, one conducted fully in accord with conscience. And, as Thomas says, a correct conscience "binds absolutely."[7]

But of course deviations and mistakes at various points are possible. If, for example, one reasons conscientiously, accurately, and consistently from first principles, but for some reason chooses not to act on the recommendation despite the visitation of pangs of guilt, one has what Thomas calls a "weak conscience." Or a person may make cognitive and logical mistakes in instructing the will. One may, in one of Thomas's more outrageous examples, properly intend to observe the moral rule against adultery but in the act of sexual intercourse mistake another woman for one's wife! Or one may mistakenly believe with the heretics that God regards all oaths as wrong; or, still again, one may do something under the false impression that it will have good effects. Finally, one may have reasoned fallaciously in arriving at certain particular conclusions.

People who make mistakes of this sort have erroneous consciences. The error involved may be culpable or inculpable, depending on whether it is the result of negligence or willfulness of some kind. If it is, then the mistake is inexcusable and the person making it is held responsible. But if it is not, then the person in error is held to be in "invincible ignorance" and is excused from blame. The difficulty of knowing for sure when someone is acting willfully or negligently in face of error has some important consequences for Thomas's attitude toward religious liberty and freedom of conscience, as we shall see.

In any case, an inculpably erroneous conscience is morally binding and must be respected as such. In other words, from an observer's point of view a person judged to have an erroneous conscience is still bound to follow that conscience, so long as the observer is convinced that the alleged ignorance is invincible.

This point is important for understanding the sort of freedom Thomas extends to those who hold conscientious beliefs. For Thomas, it seems that a person's will is totally dependent upon the recommendations for action put to it by the conscience. The will is above all morally bound to act upon such a recommendation, providing of course the person is conscientious. In fact, for Thomas this sort of choice by the will is the only truly *free* choice. But that means, as D'Arcy points out, that *"if reason presents an [inculpably] false picture, the will cannot be blamed;* there is only one standard for judging it: *the good as apprehended [by reason].* If [the will] fails to live up to that, its only standard, its performance is bad. But if it is faithful to its only standard, its performance is surely good."[8] The argument obviously moves in the direction of tolerating conscientiously held beliefs and actions with which one may profoundly disagree.

The argument becomes sharpened somewhat in specific reference to religious belief. To begin with, Thomas claims that unbelievers who have never been Catholics must not be coerced into joining the church.

The argument is very simple. The act of faith is essentially a free act; without an interior, free choice of the will there is no valid act of faith at all. It is therefore not lawful to use compulsion in any way to force Jews or pagans to accept the Christian faith. With regard to making the initial act of faith, St. Thomas accepts St. Augustine's principle, "A person can do other things against his will; but belief is possible only in one who is willing." A man may sign a contract, join a firing squad, pronounce an oath of allegiance, without any interior consent; but *unwilling belief is an impossibility. The only valid act of faith is that which proceeds from a free, interior choice.*[9]

And Thomas is thoroughly consistent on this point: "Belief in Christ is, of itself, something good, and necessary for salvation. But if one's reason presented it as something evil, one's will would be doing wrong in adopting it."[10] This is a particularly arresting statement. Thomas clearly asserts that it is conceivable for someone to reject Christian belief *blamelessly,* at least from a human point of view, because of invincible ignorance. The Christian will not agree with the nonbeliever, but should nevertheless honor the conscientiousness of unbelief and forbear any coercive intervention. Deep matters of conscience are beyond a human outsider's control; they are so profoundly private and personal that they are strictly between the individual and God. It should be added that Thomas does permit force against uninitiated unbelievers, but only as defensive counterforce against persecution. Unprovoked coercion against peaceful unbelievers would not be justified.

In many ways this is a remarkable view for the intellectual leader of the church of the High Middle Ages to have held. Its implications are quite radical. But Thomas did not see those implications through. In fact, he seems to have contradicted them at several points. For example, he drew a sharp distinction between uninitiated unbelievers, on the one hand, and apostates and heretics, on the other. While the first group might not be coerced against their consciences, the second group could be. Heretics and apostates, Thomas writes, "at one time accepted the faith, and professed it; they must be compelled even by physical force, to carry out what they promised and to hold what they once accepted."[11] The argument is that promises once made may be enforced by the state, if necessary. This case therefore constitutes an exception in Thomas's mind to tolerating ordinary unbelievers.

It is important to notice, in passing, that Thomas's argument in favor of this sort of exception is not very convincing. If it is wrong, as he argues, to will to believe, or to act as though one did believe in Christ, when one's reason presents that belief as something mistaken, then it is surely wrong on Thomas's own terms to go on willing in that way if for some reason one has ceased to believe or has changed one's beliefs.

The matter of freedom of religion and conscience was left in this state of ambiguity up through the Renaissance and Reformation, and well into the seventeenth and eighteenth centuries in England and America, where modern formulations were eventually worked out.

Of special importance in the development of Anglo-American notions of religious liberty was the Calvinist or Reformed side of the Reformation, a tradition that displays the tension between uniformity and diversity in religious belief and practice with particular force. Partly influenced by Renaissance humanism, "one of the great strands in the fabric of liberty,"[12] and partly by medieval and sectarian Christian views of conscience, Calvin placed freedom of conscience at the center of his theological concerns.[13] In doing so he intensified some of the complexities and inconsistencies surrounding the notion in the history of Christian reflection on the subject.

Generally speaking, Calvin's thought was an unstable amalgam of sectarian, Anabaptist themes—a voluntary, consensual community; an elevated sense of personal, lay responsibility in religious and moral life; and a sharp limitation on civil authority—together with certain medieval Catholic themes—an established, uniform church and civilly enforceable religious supervision of all aspects of social life.[14]

The sectarian tradition characteristically radicalized the idea of free conscience that is, as we have shown, deeply embedded in the Christian tradition. For the sectarians the ultimate purpose of religious and civil life was to protect and provide opportunity for the genuine expression of free conscience, and there is much in Calvin's thought and practice that exhibits this strong sectarian tone. For example, he placed great emphasis upon the distinction between the "inner forum," or "forum of conscience," and the "earthly forum," or human government:

> There is a twofold government in man: one aspect is spiritual, whereby the conscience is instructed in piety and reverencing God; the second is political, whereby man is educated for the duties of humanity and citizenship that must be maintained among men. These are usually called the "spiritual" and "temporal" jurisdiction . . . by which is meant that the former sort of government pertains to the life of the soul, while the latter has to do with the concerns of the present life—not only with food and clothing but with laying down laws whereby a man may live his life among other men holily, honorably and temperately. For the former resides in the inner mind, while the latter regulates only outward behavior. The one we may call the spiritual kingdom, the other, the political kingdom. Now these two, as we have divided them, must always be examined separately; and while one is being considered, we must call away and turn aside the mind from thinking about the other. There are in man, so to speak, two worlds, over which different kings and different laws have authority.[15]

It is this basic distinction between "the life of the soul," of the inner mind, "whereby the conscience is instructed in piety and reverencing God," and the life of political, "outward behavior" that accounts for the sharp line Calvin draws in keeping with sectarian sentiments between "the law of the spirit" and "the law of the sword" (4.9.3).

At bottom, it is in the nature of the conscience, of the inner mind, to conduct itself according to rules and requirements that operate independent of physical coercion and punishment such as "the magistrate commonly inflicts." And unless the conscience is allowed to perform in accord with its nature, allowed, that is, to function without harassment and "chastisement" from the civil authority, it will not have fulfilled its purpose. Accordingly, Calvin reasserts the venerable Christian emphasis upon the indispensability of free exercise in respect to the fundamental matters of the inner life.

Calvin draws the distinction between the inner and outer life, again consistent with a sectarian emphasis, as an expression of the two different tables of the Decalogue. Commandments one through four mark the "religious" duties owed directly to God, and commandments five through ten mark the "moral" duties owed to fellow human beings. The underlying assumption is that in respect to "heavenly things," or matters pertaining to the first table (pure knowledge of God, the nature of true righteousness, and the mysteries of the heavenly kingdom), "human knowledge wholly fails" (2.2.24), and thus explicit divine intervention and enlightenment is required. In other words, the religious sphere is reserved for direct divine regulation, a condition that in theory preempts all exercise of human authority, including civil authority.

By contrast, in respect to "earthly affairs," or matters of the second table (human government, household management, mechanical skills, and the liberal arts), "there exist in all men's minds universal impressions of a certain civic fair dealing and order"; some seed of political order has been implanted in all men. And this is ample proof that in the arrangement of this life no man is without the light of reason" (2.2.13). Consequently, "men have somewhat more [natural] understanding of the precepts of the Second Table [than the first] because these are more closely concerned with the preservation of civil society among them" (2.2.24). It follows for Calvin that the exercise of human authority—including, of course, the use of physical coercion and punishment—is fully appropriate in the "moral sphere."

However, there is another side to Calvin's thought that is representative of the establishmentarian, medieval Catholic tradition, a side that in many ways conflicts with the sectarian emphasis upon freedom of religion and conscience. Having laid it down in no uncertain terms that the "spiritual kingdom" and the "political kingdom" "must always be examined separately"—"while one is being considered, we must call away and turn aside the mind from thinking about the other"—Calvin promptly appears to disregard what he has said:

> We must know that [the two kingdoms] are not at variance. For spiritual government, indeed, is already initiating in us upon earth certain beginnings of the Heavenly Kingdom, and in this mortal and fleeting life affords a certain forecast of an immortal and incorruptible blessedness. Yet civil government has as its appointed end, so long as we live among men, to cherish and protect the outward worship of God, to defend sound doctrine of piety and the position of the church, to adjust our life to the society of men, to form our social behavior to civil righteousness, to reconcile us with one another, and to promote general peace and tranquility (4.20.2).

Whereas on the first view the exercise of civil authority should be thoroughly restricted to the enforcement of moral and civil concerns, and not interfere at all in the religious sphere, here Calvin unmistakably warrants an extensive intermingling of the two spheres by authorizing civil government to enforce worship and sound doctrine. These two incompatible theories of the relation between the spiritual and the temporal orders, theories that struggle against each other in Calvin's thought as well as in the development of the several varieties of Calvinism, lead, predictably, to conflicting conclusions concerning the Calvinist doctrine of erroneous conscience.

The "sectarian" strand entails a widely permissive attitude toward religious belief and practice. If conscience must be allowed to function free of human and external encumbrances, then people must be at liberty, so long as they honor the physical and material well-being of others, to adopt and act upon religious beliefs as they see fit. That means that from any one religious perspective contrary views will often appear erroneous, and sometimes seriously so. But however sharp the disagreements, they must be borne in the name of the free determination of religious conviction. Religion that is not voluntarily embraced is no religion at all.

This is in fact the implication of one of the key features of Calvin's notion of freedom of conscience. It is that "consciences observe [God's] law, not as if constrained by the necessity of the law, but that freed from the law's yoke *they willingly obey God's will*" (3.29.4; emphasis added). To give so much prominence as Calvin does to the opportunity for an "eager readiness to obey God" logically requires an equivalent opportunity to think and behave in a different way, for by definition eager readiness must come from the heart; it cannot be compelled. In consequence, believers ought to be ready to bear with or suffer widely diverse responses to religious claims without interfering coercively.

However, the other side of Calvin's thought hardly moves in such a permissive direction. When Calvin comes explicitly to discuss the subject of erroneous conscience, he is considerably more restrictive than the above conclusions would suggest. He declares that religious error is tolerable in "things indifferent," though never in essential matters of doctrine and worship (3.19.13). For example, anyone advocating the "papal mass" ought never be tolerated because such a practice constitutes, from the point of view of Reformed doctrine, a direct assault upon (what was to Calvin) manifestly true and essential faith. On the other hand, Calvin was willing to permit diversity among people of conscience concerning what he considered to be peripheral questions of faith and worship (3.19.7ff).

Contrary to the implications of the first view, according to which civil authority might regulate civil and moral, but not religious, matters, this second view encourages elaborate civil enforcement of "things essential" in religion. Accordingly, whereas the first view distinguishes rather sharply between the "religious" and "moral" tables of the Decalogue, the second view interconnects them, with the strong suggestion that "civic fair dealing and order" depend directly upon a uniform and enforced orthodoxy.

This deep tension within Calvin's thought over the subject of freedom of religion and conscience exhibited itself with particular force and significance in the debates over church-state relations among Calvinists in seventeenth-century colonial New England. The uniformist strand was represented by John Cotton, the intrepid defender of the Massachusetts Bay religious establishment, while the sectarian, liberal cause was taken up by Roger Williams. Because of his beliefs Williams was exiled from Massachusetts Bay, and eventually founded the Rhode Island colony as an early and remarkable experiment in religious freedom. The essential point of contention was over the proper interpretation and institutionalization of freedom of conscience and religion, and the terms and arguments of the extended controversy between the two men were simply variations, respectively, upon the basic inconsistencies in Calvin's thought.[16]

In reply to Williams's ardent criticisms of what he took to be the rank intolerance of Massachusetts Bay, Cotton answers characteristically:

> The fundamentals [of true religion] are so clear, that a man cannot but be convinced of the truth of them after two or three admonitions; and that, therefore, such a person as still continues obstinate is condemned of himself. And if he

then be punished, he is not punished for his conscience, but for sinning against his own conscience. . . .

God in times past suffered all nations to walk in their own ways. And so did His vicegerents, the good kings of Israel, do the like. David did not compel the tributary nations to worship the God of Israel. No more does our colony here compel the tributary Indians to worship our God. But if an Israelite forsakes God, he disturbs not only the Commonwealth of Israel, but the barks of pagans and heathen states, as Jonah did this ship by his departure from God. Therefore, a Christian by departing from God may disturb a gentile civil state. And it is no preposterous way for the governors of the state, according to the quality of the disturbance raised by the starting aside of such a Christian, to punish both it and him by civil censure.[17]

Moreover, Cotton, following certain central themes in Calvin's thought, links religion and morality very closely. Apostasy and heresy, it seems, inevitably produce moral violations. "Never look for true dealing from an heretic that lies against the Gospel, and against his own conscience; never believe any doctrine of theirs, for they aim at subverting. If they deal not truly with God, they will not deal truly with man."[18] As we shall see, Cotton's arguments here find parallels, in some important ways, in Islamic doctrine.

For his part Williams did little more than take up the liberal arguments on behalf of freedom of religion and conscience embedded in the teachings of Thomas Aquinas and Calvin and press them with relentless rigor against Cotton and the Massachusetts establishment. To begin with, Calvin and Williams, like Thomas, believed that conscience was the seat of individual freedom and sovereignty. Conscience properly acted as a private monitor in respect to the basic beliefs and the practical guidance that followed from those beliefs. Again with Thomas and Calvin, one was truly free only when one's will was allowed to be bound by the dictates of conscience. In fact, conscience is not something one can altogether help. It constrains a person often beyond one's immediate wishes and preferences. And yet conscience compels with the force of authority; it has in some deep sense the individual's final and free consent. It is not, therefore, like other compulsions that pathologically drive us against our "better judgment." As with Thomas and Calvin, conscience involves and integrates all aspects of the self: reason, will, and the affections.

Accordingly, there is established a presumption against outside interference, especially of the coercive sort. Williams's view is thoroughly (liberal) Thomist and Calvinist here: "Unwilling belief is an impossibility." To try to determine an individual's basic commitments, or to disturb the practical inferences conscientiously drawn from them, by means of compulsion is an affront to the fundamental structure of the self.

Actually Williams is doing little more here than tightening up and taking the consequences of one way of interpreting the notion of erroneous conscience. Williams had his own decided theological convictions, which were strongly, if sometimes deviantly, Calvinist. He did not agree with the religious views of the American Indians or "pagans," as he called them, nor with the "Mohammedans," nor "Papists," nor many other Protestants, such as the Quakers. He frequently and in detail made known his objections to some of these groups; he regarded many of them as seriously in error. But for all the above reasons *they had a right to their error.* Because of what Thomas called invincible ignorance they were excused from punishment and compulsion in matters of religious belief and practice. As Williams put it in an interesting remark: "This conscience is found in all mankind, more or less [more or less erroneously, that is], in Jews, Turks, papists, Protestants, pagans, etc." and ought to be respected accordingly.[19]

As we see, none of this is particularly new. Williams's signal innovation in respect to modern formulations of liberty of conscience is to tie all this to the crucial distinction between morality and religion illustrated by the contrast between the two tables of the Decalogue. Initially, even this move is not totally at odds with Thomas and Calvin. Williams affirms the existence of certain fundamental moral truths that he assumes are objectively and universally binding. They constitute the natural law that is imprinted upon the human psyche. Thomas would have called these the constitutive features of *synderesis*, and in Calvin's view these truths are the moral law "engraved upon the minds of men." For Williams they are the fundamental requirements of social cooperation: nonmaleficence, truth-telling and promise-keeping, at least limited beneficence (duty of mutual aid), and a standard of justice and reciprocity. In addition, Williams assumes some standard canons of reasonableness and conscientiousness, according to which the application of these basic moral duties may be assessed.[20]

These natural-moral duties are, so to speak, the inalterable conditions of conscience and will. The systematic repudiation of any one of them could not be an act of conscience or "free will." Deliberately to inflict severe suffering and injury upon an innocent person for the fun of it, or for other purely self-serving reasons, has to be regarded as always and everywhere wrong. The interpretation and application of these basic duties may of course vary, but Williams assumes a fixed, commonly recognizable core. For this reason these duties may properly be enforced by the state. They establish the basis for what Williams called the "law civil and moral."

The underlying idea here is beautifully symmetrical. Because certain basic "moral" violations of the second-table sort—unlawful killing, theft, or libel—themselves involve coercion or severe bodily injury, therefore equivalent countermeasures in the form of civil coercion and injury are justified and appropriate, either to prevent or to punish such violations. By contrast, since "religious" belief, about God or the superempirical world, properly "proceeds [for all human beings] from a free interior choice," such belief is *not* appropriately counterbalanced by coercion or other external forms of control, but only by another belief.

Consequently the only beliefs and practices that may permissibly be met by coercion are those, either religious or moral, that inspire or produce the basic sort of "moral" violations mentioned above. The conscience is therefore controlled in its operations by these basic moral constraints against arbitrary violence or injury. So long as it remains "in bounds," as well as measures up to the requirements of conscientious deliberation, the conscience is free to go about its business. Again, exactly where the line is to be drawn regarding basic moral violations of course varies throughout the tradition. Therefore the range of permissibly punishable actions naturally varies also. Still, all parties in the Christian tradition operate within this same fundamental framework and are wrestling with the same basic problem.

There is increasing evidence that Williams's application of Christian teaching provided an important part of the intellectual framework and fundamental principles according to which the American doctrine of liberty of conscience and religion was worked out in the eighteenth century by Thomas Jefferson and James Madison. Jefferson's Statute for Religious Freedom, adopted by the Virginia Legislature in 1786, and Madison's Memorial and Remonstrance against Religious Assessments, published in 1785 in indirect support of the Statute, cannot be understood apart from the arguments so forcefully articulated by Williams and picked up and conveyed to Jefferson and Madison by figures like John Locke and, later, the Separate Baptist Isaac Backus.[21]

In making their case Jefferson and Madison invoke the central distinctions and draw some of the same conclusions that are connected with the doctrine of erroneous conscience, and particularly with Williams's deployment of that doctrine. For example, they mark out firm lines between the "internal forum" and the "external forum," and seek to protect the former from the latter by guaranteeing all citizens' natural civil and political rights, whatever their religious opinions. Madison writes:

> Because we hold it for a fundamental and undeniable truth, "that Religion or the duty which we owe to our Creator and the manner of discharging it, can be

directed only by reason and conviction, not by force or violence." The Religion then of every man must be left to the conviction and conscience of every man; and it is the right of every man to exercise it as these may dictate. This right is in its nature an unalienable right.[22]

Similarly, in Jefferson's words:

[Well aware] that our civil rights have no dependence on our religious opinions, more than our opinions in physics or geometry; that, therefore, the proscribing any citizen as unworthy [of] the public confidence by laying upon him an incapacity of being called to the offices of trust and emolument, unless he profess or renounce this or that religious opinion, is depriving him injuriously of those privileges and advantages to which in common with his fellow citizens he has a natural right; . . . that it is time enough for the rightful purposes of civil government, for its offices to interfere when principles break out into overt acts against peace and good order.[23]

Moreover, like Williams, Jefferson and Madison contend that enforced religion contradicts and perverts the essential voluntariness of genuine religious commitment, and that therefore the errors tolerated under a system of religious liberty are as nothing compared with the hypocrisy and corruption that is generated where religion is imposed by the civil authority.[24] Finally, Madison and Jefferson devoutly agree with Williams's belief that age-old attempts to enforce religion, having constituted "the chiefest sparks and bellows . . . in raising the devouring flames of fire and sword,"[25] are an arbitrary and impermissible use of force, and thus contrary to the state's vocation. As Madison puts it, "Torrents of blood have been spilt in the old world, by vain attempts of the secular arm, to extinguish Religious discord, by proscribing all difference in Religious opinion."[26] Jefferson echoes the same sentiments in his *Notes on Virginia:* "Is [religious] uniformity attainable? Millions of innocent men, women, and children, since the introduction of Christianity, have been burnt, tortured, fined, imprisoned; yet we have not advanced one inch toward uniformity. What has been the effect of coercion? To make one half the world fools, and the other half hypocrites."[27]

There can be little question that these expressions of religious liberty and freedom of conscience developed by Jefferson and Madison, and done so against the background of the history of the doctrine of erroneous conscience in the West, provided the model for contemporary statements. The formulations contained in Article 18 of the Universal Declaration of Human Rights and in the International Covenant on Civil and Political Rights, as well as in the Preamble and eight articles of the UN Declaration on the Elimination of

All Forms of Intolerance and Discrimination Based on Religion or Belief, are unthinkable apart from that tradition.

Our summary observations about the development in the West of the concept of conscience and its right to freedom yield the following conclusions. To conceive of the individual person as a spiritually free being who is, within wide limits, accorded sovereignty over mind, conscience, and spirit is to believe that human beings are ultimately self-guiding actors, or "agents," and not merely acted upon, that they are purposeful and deliberative rather than simply passive, externally determined creatures. It is to believe that the right to religious freedom and conscience rests upon the deep conviction that human beings are fulfilled in being guided by "reasons" and by persuasion, rather than by external "causes" and controls. In short, to conceive of human beings in terms of an indefeasible "right to freedom of thought, conscience, religion and belief," in the words of the Declaration against Intolerance, is itself to affirm and to seek to guarantee the "natural" irreducibility of the human spirit.

There is even the implication, suggested by the distinction between the "religious" and "moral" commandments, that whatever else it may mean, to have a religion or to be religious is to be committed to the idea that human beings live in two worlds at the same time, two worlds that are never completely harmonious and never completely reducible to each other. Moreover, there is the suggestion that to be religious is to be committed to the idea that human consciousness, and the laws of reason and spirit by which that consciousness operates, are not simply the extension of or interpretable by the laws of cause and effect that appear to govern the nonhuman world. In other words, according to our survey, to be religious is to know and to mark well, in some terms or other, the difference between the laws of the "internal forum" and the laws of the "external forum."

A Proposal for Comparing the World's Religions

It is time to draw together our proposal for comparing the world's religions. It amounts to this: On the basis of accumulated experience in the West in considering the subject of the freedom of religion and conscience, it is reasonable to extend our thinking. It is reasonable to do that because Western experience appears to illuminate central features of the world's religions every bit as much as it does those of Western Christianity, and may therefore be expected to "ring bells" in other traditions.

The basic idea is that the very concept of religion is premised on what we might call "the puzzle of the human person." That puzzle enshrouds any attempt to provide a satisfactory and complete explanation or account of the origins and operations of human consciousness and self-identity. Our proposal suggests that believers we would ordinarily call religious (the world around) will be discovered to be fundamentally committed to some version of the irreducibility of human consciousness and personal identity.

That is, religious believers will, as a central part of their belief system, hold to what we may call a double-minded distinction between two sorts of laws of behavior—spiritual and material, inner and outer, sacred and profane, real and illusory, extraordinary and ordinary, otherworldly and this-worldly, or some such. In addition, they will hold that the distinction is inalterable, indeed that it is constitutive of life itself, and accordingly that the spiritual or inner or "real" world may never be reduced to, nor completely controlled or explained by, the material or outer or "illusory" world.

According to this way of putting it, then, we approach the world's religions expecting that the double-mindedness we speak of, and all it represents regarding a response to our puzzle, will be found to resonate right down to the foundations of the various sacred traditions.

Furthermore, the attendant dilemmas we identified in this survey will also, we would expect, be found at the center of the experience and the struggles of the various traditions. The tension between spirit and coercion, between the inner and outer forum, appears, it seems obvious, to be but a specification of the more general distinction between two sorts of laws of behavior that is, as suggested, central to religious experience.

Finally, the tension between morality and religion, as we described it, is but another way of exhibiting the same underlying puzzle. It is, we saw, nothing more than the polarity between the "moral" laws recommended to regulate acts of physical force or severe injury—acts of external causation— and the laws that are believed to govern free or spiritual encounter, namely the laws of interior or "religious" life.

The different religions of the world will no doubt respond differently to the common points of orientation and the common problems, and to an important extent precisely those differences will constitute crucial divergences and areas of contention among them. Still, if it is commonly applicable in the way suggested, then the proposal helps to establish the fact that the members of the world's religions are all potentially partners in a grand intercultural "multilogue" to be organized around the shared points of reference.

Presumably, therefore, members of the various traditions will begin to look afresh at their own traditions as well as at the traditions of others in the light of our proposal. However the participants may decide to cope with their differences, they will come at least to recognize that they are partners in a common discussion. That in itself would be no mean achievement.

The Case of Islam

If it is relatively easy to point to the utility and applicability of our framework to other religions such as Buddhism, Islam poses, it would seem, a harder case and therefore constitutes a more strenuous test for our endeavor. Troeltsch, for one, regarded Buddhism as peculiarly compatible with Christianity; but Islam, he thought, was not very compatible because, as a "religion of the law," its resources for differentiating between the inner[28] and outer, or the spiritual and civil, realms are relatively underdeveloped. Troeltsch's impression still seems to be a prevalent one, even among some Muslims and students of Islam.[29]

But this impression is, we believe, profoundly one-sided. There is warrant for suggesting that Islam too conforms to the expectations generated by our framework. It is certainly not difficult to show that Islam, like other of the world's religions, postulates a foundational division between two sorts of laws of behavior—"the ways of Allah," on the one hand, and "the ways of the world," on the other. The more sensitive question is whether the ways of Allah, after all, are systemically conceived in reference to a belief in the irreducible differentiation of the human person from this-worldly causes and constraints. In other words, is there a law of the spirit, of the inner life, that from an Islamic point of view is sharply distinguished from the laws of the outer, including civil, life?

The answer is, we suggest, affirmative, a verdict that has the most important consequences for understanding the idea of religious freedom in Islam. Just because there is strong evidence in the Qur'an that true religious belief is a deeply inward and personal matter, a matter of the heart, there are firm grounds for several quite unexpected affirmations in the Qur'an of religious tolerance and forbearance. There is, to begin with, Sura 109, "The Unbelievers":

> Say: "O unbelievers,
> I serve not what you serve
> and you are not serving what I serve,
> nor am I serving what you have served,
> neither are you serving what I serve.
> To you your religion, and to me my religion."

Even more pointedly, the Qur'an states, "No compulsion is there in religion" (2:256)—words that begin to make one think of the emphasis placed by Thomas Aquinas, John Calvin, and Roger Williams upon the irreducible voluntariness of religious belief. In fact, the Qur'an stresses that an individual's spiritual destiny is strictly between that person and Allah. Other people, including Muhammad, have no power to alter coercively an individual's religious beliefs, nor, for that matter, any responsibility to try. Presumably genuine submission or surrender to Allah's will, along with the appropriate dispositions of gratitude, devotion, steadfastness, etc., must come from the heart, must involve the deepest and most intimate kind of personal consent and commitment. If that is true, then compulsion and external interference would appear to be the antithesis of Islamic faith. The Qur'an says as much:

Had God willed, they were not idolaters;
and *We have not appointed thee a watcher over them,
neither art thou their guardian* (6:108; emphasis added).

Those who have made divisions in their religion and become sects, thou art not of them in anything; *their affair is unto God,* then He will tell them what they have been doing (6:160; emphasis added).

And if thy Lord had willed, whoever is in the earth would have believed, all of them, all together. *Wouldst thou then constrain the people, until they are believers* (10:99; emphasis added).

There is even a suggestion in the Qur'an of a version of the parable of the wheat and the tares in the New Testament, a parable that was dear to the heart of Roger Williams.

So we have appointed to every Prophet an enemy—
Satans of men and jinn, revealing tawdry
speech to each other, all as a delusion;
yet, had thy Lord willed, they would never
have done it. So leave them to their forging (6:113).

The material is thoroughly compatible with the notion of erroneous conscience that is so central to the Western tradition. The Qur'an leaves no doubt in these passages that it regards idolaters as profoundly in error. However, "their case will go to Allah." They are, it would appear, thereby excused from punishment, compulsion, and other civil disabilities in relation to their religious beliefs and practices.

But how then shall we explain the obvious references in the Qur'an to the use of force in regard to idolaters and unbelievers? A careful review of the context in which such references occur reveals that the only permissible use of force is defensive. That is, if non-Muslims themselves *initiate* the use of force for purposes of military conquest or religious persecution, or in breach of a solemn treaty, *then and only then,* it would appear, is forceful reaction justifiable. In other words, if this description is accurate, then the distinction as well as the symmetries we alluded to earlier between "morality" and "religion" are very much in play here.

The Qur'an frequently justifies coercion and punishment against apostates and even some unbelievers, in retaliation for breaking their agreement of covenant with the forces of Muhammad (and thus with Allah). Sura 9 is particularly clear here, but 4:89 indicates that force is justified "if they turn back [to enmity]" (Pickthall's translation). The same seems true of 2:216–218. Those passages justify force as retaliation for persecution and the threat of destruction. These are all presumably appeals to basic moral requirements—either to keep promises and treaties, or to protect a community's basic welfare and security against aggression. So construed, these injunctions to use force against unbelievers are grounded in emergency conditions, which consist of moral rather than religious provocations. That is, it is not primarily because the unbelievers hold the beliefs they do, but because of their manifest moral violations, that they are liable to punishment and coercion. At least, this account appears plausible, particularly because it provides a way to combine the strong emphasis on religious freedom with the defense of compulsion against the apostates and others.

In short, forceful countermeasures against an aggressive intiation of force are "morally" justified by conditions that are believed to bind all human beings, regardless of religious identity or affiliation. Indeed, there appears to be a compelling analogue in the Qur'an to the Western notion of natural moral law, which also yields similar guidance with regard to the use of force. Beyond these "natural moral" limits force would not be permissible. In particular, coercion would not be an acceptable response to what is regarded as erroneous belief and worship in matters that are strictly "religious."

This account of deep and surprising parallels between the Western and the Islamic traditions has not magically removed all tensions and strains. Even if this proposal is correct—that the Islamic tradition, like that of the West, implies a strong burden of proof upon political authorities to show cause for compulsion in religious affairs—there will still be deep differences, among other things, over what is to count as a sufficient justification in given circumstances for compulsion. What is regarded as a mortal threat in an Islamic society may not be so regarded in a Western liberal society. All that needs, in its own right, the most careful sort of exploration.

But the central point still stands: Both traditions share a common framework within which to think about freedom of conscience and religious liberty, and many of the categories are mutually applicable in a most illuminating way. Thus, current human rights formulations, along with the important notions that underlie them, are by no means necessarily irrelevant to cultures outside the West. Granted, similarities between just two traditions does not prove anything to the universally true. But it is a start.

NOTES

1. C. A. Pierce, *Conscience in the New Testament* (London: SCM Press, 1955), 21–22; emphasis added.

2. Pierce, *Conscience*, 42–43.

3. Eric D'Arcy, *Conscience and Its Right to Freedom* (London: Sheed & Ward, 1961), 7–8.

4. John Kelsay, unpublished paper, "Thoughts on the Pauline Understanding of Conscience."

5. See Timothy C. Potts, *Conscience in Medieval Philosophy* (Cambridge: Cambridge University Press, 1980).

6. Thomas discusses his theory of conscience in three places: *Commentary on the Sentences of Peter Lombard: de Veritate*, Questions 16 and 17; and *Summa Theologica* 1:79. I am indebted to D'Arcy's excellent treatment of Thomas's notion of conscience (*Conscience and Its Rights to Freedom*), though the framework just suggested is my own.

7. *de Veritate*, Q. 17, art. 4.

8. D'Arcy, *Conscience*, 117–18; emphasis added.

9. D'Arcy, *Conscience*, 160, 153–54; emphasis added.

10. *Summa Theologica* 1-2.19, 5.

11. Cited by D'Arcy, *Conscience*, 159.

12. Roland Bainton, *The Travail of Religious Liberty* (Philadelphia: Westminster Press, 1951), 57.

13. Calvin develops his notion of conscience particularly in the *Institutes of the Christian Religion*, 3.19 and 4.10. His *Commentary on Romans* (2:14–15) should also be consulted. See David Little, *Religion, Order, and Law* (Chicago: University of Chicago Press, 1984), 50–56; Little has developed Calvin's theory of conscience more fully in an unpublished paper, "Is Support for the Santuary Movement Justified? A Contemporary 'Case of Conscience' in the Light of Reformed Christianity."

14. Ernst Troeltsch makes this case in his treatment of Calvin in *Social Teachings of the Christian Churches* (London: Allen & Unwin, 1956), 2:590–602. Cf. Little, *Religion, Order and Law*, 75–80.

15. Calvin, *Institutes of the Christian Religion* (Philadelphia: Westminster Press, 1960), 3,19,15. Further references to the *Institutes* will be given parenthetically in the text.

16. Little has explicated the Calvinist background of the tensions between Cotton and Williams in "Reformed Faith and Religious Liberty," *Church and Society* (May/June, 1986), 5–28, and in an unpublished essay, "Reflections on the Fortunes of Religious Liberty from the Thirteenth to the Seventeenth Centuries in Europe and America." This essay is a critical response to

the arguments of Quentin Skinner (*Foundations of Modern Political Thought*) and Jeffrey Stout (*Flight from Authority*) concerning the origins and rise of religious liberty and freedom of conscience in the West. Their contention that a belief in these things is chiefly the result of pragmatic compromise in face of religious conflict completely overlooks the background out of which these beliefs emerged. For a more concentrated discussion of Williams's ideas, see Little, "Roger Williams and the Separation of Church and State," *Religion and the State*, ed. James E. Wood (Waco, Tex.: Baylor University Press, 1985), 3–23.

17. Cited in Irwin Polishhook, ed., *Roger Williams, John Cotton and Religious Freedom* (Englewood Cliffs, N.J.: Prentice-Hall, 1967), 72–73.

18. Polishhook, *Roger Williams*, 77.

19. *Complete Writings of Roger Williams*, 7 vols. (New York: Russell & Russell, 1963), 4:508.

20. Perry Miller has emphasized Williams's devotion to "rational argument" in *Roger Williams: His Contributions to the American Tradition* (New York: Atheneum, 1962), 243, though the subject of Williams's appeals to reason in religious and moral argument awaits thorough investigation.

21. See Little, "Roger Williams and the Separation of Church and State," and "Religion and American Civil Life: Jefferson's Statute Reconsidered," *Virginia Statute for Religious Freedom: Its Evolution and Consequences in American History*, eds. Merrill Paterson and Robert Vaughan (Cambridge: Cambridge University Press, 1988).

22. James Madison, "A Memorial and Remonstrance Against Religious Assessments," in Joseph A. Blau, ed., *Cornerstones of Religious Freedom in America* (New York: Harper, 1964), 84.

23. *Life and Selected Writings of Thomas Jefferson*, ed. Adrienne Koch and William Peden (New York: Modern Library, 1944), 312–13.

24. See Preamble to the Statute, *Life and Writings of Jefferson*, 311, and Madison, "Memorial," 301.

25. Williams, *Complete Writings*, 4:328.

26. Madison, "Memorial," 302.

27. *Life and Writings of Jefferson*, 276.

28. Troeltsch, *Absoluteness of Christianity*, 109ff.

29. E.g. Piscatori, "Human Rights in Islamic Culture," *Moral Imperative of Human Rights*, ed. Kenneth W. Thompson (Washington: University Press of America, 1980), and Max Stackhouse (see note 2, ch. 2 below).

2. Saudi Arabia, Pakistan, and the Universal Declaration of Human Rights

Much has been written about the relation of Islam and Islamic culture to Western notions concerning the organization of society and human rights. And, one must admit, the point of much of this writing has been to say that, *contra* our suggestions thus far, Islam and the West are at opposite poles with respect to these important issues. Thus Adda Bozeman concludes that Islamic culture is *not* guided by notions of right or principle, as the West understands them. Instead, Islamic culture is characterized by the governance of personalism and pragmatism, where ruling authority is "illegitimate and coercive almost by definition."[1] Similarly, Max Stackhouse, author of a recent study of human rights in three cultures, has indicated that Islam is a religious tradition ill suited to democratic conceptions of society. It simply does not present the individual with those opportunities for freedom of action and association that are characteristic of Western Christianity (in certain cases).[2] Even an author who concludes, as James Piscatori does, that the respect for life and property which Islam teaches and its practice of tolerance and fraternity indicate that it "unquestionably shares much of the spirit of the present human rights movement," can also say that Islam "does not advance the basic idea of inalienable rights, nor does it avoid distinguishing according to sex and religion." In short, "Islamic theory does not present a notion of the rights of the individual. Rights do not attach to men *qua* men. . . . It is more appropriate to refer to the *privileges* of man."[3]

Given such evidence, what is one to think of the proposal advanced above, to the effect that Islam and the West have much to talk about in relation to human rights and freedom of conscience? If one follows Bozeman and Stackhouse, for example, it seems that our dialogue is over before it has begun!

33

And while Piscatori's discussion is more nuanced, his findings indicate that the best one can hope for is a limited exchange. This is so particularly with respect to the issues of freedom of conscience with which this study is concerned.

However, a closer examination of the arguments of Bozeman and others reveals a gap of major import, given a desire to discuss such issues in "dialogical" fashion. This "gap" consists in the failure to pay attention to what participants in Islamic culture have to say about human rights, especially freedom of conscience. Or, even when there is some attention to Islamic "self-statement," as in Piscatori's article, it is limited to the point of view of one school or party within Islam. It is plain enough that Western culture is characterized by diverse perspectives on issues of human rights. Should one not expect a similar diversity within other world cultures? And how is one to evaluate this expectation without more extensive attention being paid to the statements of representatives of these cultures?

This discussion of Islam and religious liberty begins, then, with the stipulation that a dialogical approach requires a greater appreciation of the statements of Muslims on matters of human rights. Further, it is important to know the extent and nature of disagreement among representatives of Islamic culture on these matters. To that end the following discussion focuses on one example of such disagreement, involving the statements of representatives of Saudi Arabia and Pakistan at the United Nations with respect to the Universal Declaration of Human Rights (1948). The goal is to understand the different perspectives that may be connected with the tradition of Islam. The attainment of this goal will require further exploration into the history of Islam in Saudi Arabia and Pakistan, and ultimately a discussion of certain classical interpretations of the Qur'an which are related to this history.

The Universal Declaration of Human Rights: Muslim Contributions

The discussion surrounding the Universal Declaration of Human Rights at the United Nations provides a unique starting point for an inquiry concerning Islam and religious liberty. This is so because of the international nature of the discussion, and because certain articles of the Declaration address the issues connected with religious freedom directly—notably Article 18, which provides for the right to freedom of conscience in the choice and practice of religious faith, including the right to change one's religion. It was this last provision that gave rise to disagreement between the Islamic states of Saudi Arabia and Pakistan.[4]

Saudi Arabia, Pakistan, and the Universal Declaration

First, it is appropriate to note the approval, even enthusiasm, with which the possibility of a Universal Declaration of Human Rights was viewed by delegates to the United Nations in 1948. As one might expect, it was certain Western powers who exhibited such enthusiasm notably Great Britain and the United States. Eleanor Roosevelt, for example, commented on the document in terms of its potential as a Magna Carta for all people.[5] Perhaps less predictably, this enthusiastic tendency was also exemplified by delegates from nations outside the Western circle of superpowers, and even by those from non-Western countries. Indeed, nearly all those participating expressed great hopes for the document and their sense that the world was waiting to hear the new organization speak. It was felt that the Universal Declaration would be part of a new international consensus, especially related to the aftermath of the Second World War and a renewed sense of the plight of oppressed peoples. Thus, the Latin American participants spoke well of the Declaration, as did the representatives from Taiwan and several of the Middle Eastern countries. For the most part, those who expressed reservations did so in terms of specific problems related to implementation or the question of national sovereignty relative to such an international document.

A different sort of criticism was sounded, albeit cautiously, by the Saudi Arabian representative, al-Barudi. At the outset of the committee discussions he commented that the draft of the Declaration before him was based largely on the patterns of culture dominant in the West, patterns frequently "at variance with the patterns of culture of Eastern States."[6] The sort of difficulty Mr. Barudi had in mind would become apparent in the discussion of the basis of human rights (Article 1) and ultimately of religious liberty (Article 18). With respect to former, which the Declaration tied to the possession of reason and conscience, the Saudi representative "pointed out that to say that all human beings were endowed with reason and conscience was too broad a statement, one that was not, and had never been, true. Moreover, the words 'dignity and rights' used in the first sentence were ambiguous and had different meanings in different countries."[7]

The statement in Article 18, which indicated the basic freedom of human conscience in religious matters, was also troubling to Mr. Barudi. This was particularly so because freedom of conscience was construed in the article as including the right to change one's religion. Mr. Barudi requested that this article be amended, arguing that it would open the door to proselytism and political unrest—even war. Perhaps dissembling a bit, he then stated that the portion of the article which recognized the right to freedom of conscience already contained the right to change one's religion, and asked why this right then had to be stated so explicitly. In the end, the difficulty, according to Barudi, was that the right to change one's religion, at least for Muslims, was not recognized in Islamic law. Most of the Islamic countries agreed with him, and those representatives whose nations contained large percentages of Muslims, yet who voted for the provision, were castigated by the Saudi representative for betraying their constituency.

Now, al-Barudi's comments on this and other issues (the rights of women, for example) are not surprising, given the literature cited at the outset of this chapter. Indeed, the Saudi representative's statements serve as an important source in Piscatori's discussion, and seem to be consistent with the idea that Islamic culture is opposed to much of what is signified by the notion of human rights, in relation to Western culture.

But al-Barudi was not the only one to comment on the relation between the provisions of Article 18 and Islam. So far as the committee hearings on the draft Declaration are concerned, one fails to notice any significant divergence from or disagreement with the Saudi position among the Islamic countries. But when the Declaration came before the General Assembly for a final vote, Pakistan's Mohammed Zafrullah Khan made a very interesting statement on the issue of religious liberty. Indeed, at certain points he appears to have intended to challenge al-Barudi directly. As the records have it, Zafrullah Khan said that

> Pakistan was an ardent defender of freedom of thought and belief and of all the freedoms listed [in Article 18]. There could be no doubt on that point, and, if that question only had a political aspect, the declaration he had just made would have been sufficient. But for the Pakistani delegation the problem had a special significance as some of its aspects involved the honour of Islam. He therefore thought it necessary to explain his delegation's point of view on the subject to the Assembly; it was a point of view arising out of the teaching of Islam.

Stating that the Qur'an was the word of God, the Pakistani foreign minister continued: "Now it stated that neither faith, nor conscience which gave birth to it, could have an obligatory character. The Koran expressly said: 'Let he who chooses to believe, believe, and he who chooses to disbelieve, disbelieve,' and it formally condemned not lack of faith but hypocrisy." Islam, he said, is a missionary religion which relies on persuasion, and which recognizes the same right of conversion for other faiths as for itself. As to this entire question of freedom of religion,

> There were other aspects of the problem, but it was not appropriate to deal with them at that stage of the work (i.e., the Committee hearings on the Universal

Declaration). His delegation considered that the essential point was to repeat that for its part the Moslem religion had unequivocally proclaimed the right to freedom of conscience and had declared itself against any kind of compulsion in matters of faith or religious practices.

In closing, "the Pakistani delegation would therefore vote for Article 19 [*sic*], and would accept no limitation on its provisions."[8] The Declaration passed 48–0, with eight abstentions (including Saudi Arabia.)

If Mr. Barudi's statements are to be expected, given the literature cited above, Zafrullah Khan's are certainly not. In view of such divergence, what is the correct view of Islam and human rights—especially the right to freedom of conscience and religion? Al-Barudi spoke on the basis of Islamic law, which according to most accounts contains strict provisions for the punishment of those who change their religion (i.e., from Islam). Zafrullah Khan also claimed to be speaking authoritatively, citing the Qur'an as the word of God.

Such divergence of opinion provides a unique opportunity to explore the relationship of Islam to religious liberty. For it suggests that, in speaking about "Islam," it is necessary to specify which Islam is under consideration. To take such care will lead to an understanding of the relation between Islam and human rights that is both more complex and richer than has heretofore been appreciated in scholarly or popular literature.

Bases of Disagreement: Unity and Diversity in the Tradition of Islam

Before such a judgment can be made, one needs to explore the sense in which Islam can be understood to justify such divergent positions. What is it about Islam, as a religious tradition, which enables al-Barudi and Zafrullah Khan to consider their positions Islamic? It should be noted that, in exploring their answers in terms of the history or tradition of Islam, I am setting aside other possible explanations of their differences—say, the need of Pakistan as a newly constituted nation to assert its unity with the Western system of democratic states, or the need of Saudi Arabia to establish itself as the moral and religious leader among Arab states in the period following the Second World War. Instead, I am choosing to emphasize the significance of a certain lineage of ideas. Or, in this case, I am emphasizing diverse aspects of the tradition of Islam as a possible explanation of the disagreement between spokesmen for Saudi Arabia and Pakistan over the provisions for religious liberty in the Universal Declaration of Human Rights.

Islam and Saudi Arabia

In our consideration of Mr. Barudi's comments and the religious context in which they make sense, we may begin by noting the integral connection between the Saudi culture or social arrangement and the Wahhabi movement. Indeed, the Wahhabi doctrine would seem the motivating force in the founding of the nation, or at least one of the forces. The Saudi nation found its original impetus in the union of Muhammad ibn 'Abd al-Wahhab's religious thought with the political and military power of the house of Sa'ud. According to the great king 'Abd al-'Aziz (d. 1953), religion was the power which enabled him to put the Saudi state on a secure foundation: his family "brought all forces that are in it (i.e., the Arabian desert) under its control and managed its administration by the virtue of the social teachings of the religion."[9] By "the religion," 'Abd al-'Aziz meant Islam as interpreted by Wahhabi religious leaders.

For purposes of this study there are three aspects of this interpretation of Islam that may be understood as correlative with al-Barudi's comments on the Universal Declaration of Human Rights. These have to do with: (1) the necessity of guidance for a humanity characterized by ignorance (and thus wrongdoing); (2) the provision that guidance is contained primarily in revealed texts (rather than in natural law, for example); and (3) the corresponding duty of those having power to establish a state dedicated to the dissemination of Islamic precepts.

1. It is characteristic of Islamic thought to make a distinction between the *jahiliyya,* or "time of ignorance," and the age of prophecy, when guidance has been made clear. At first glance, then, there is nothing unusual in Wahhabi stipulations that humanity is ignorant and forgetful, and in need of a guidance that can set its members on the straight path.

What is of interest in connection with al-Barudi's statements regarding Article 18—particularly his indication that the libertarian thrust of this article would lead to civil strife—is the way that Wahhabi doctrine appears to regard the establishment of the Saudi regime as the victory of Islam over the forces of ignorance: "Know that the people of Najd—nomad and settled—before the Shaikh al-Islam (Muhammad b. 'Abd al-Wahhab) . . . were in the *jahiliyya.* Islam had become almost unknown. Evil, corruption, *shirk,* and *kufr* were widespread in towns, villages, cities, and among the desert and the sown. Idols and images were widespread. The people had abandoned *zakat.*"[10] The effective point of such an account, in conjunction with other statements of Wahhabi teaching, seems to be that the time of ignorance was a reality in pre-Wahhabi (and thus pre-Saudi) Arabia. This was so despite years of the influence of Islamic teaching and despite the fact that most of the inhabitants of the Arabian Peninsula were Sunni Muslims.

2. How could it be the case that, over 1,100 years after the life of the Prophet, the people of the Arabian Peninsula could be in the *jahiliyya*? In part, the answer is that the victory of guidance over ignorance is never complete. Or, to put it another way, the time of ignorance is not simply the pre-Islamic era, but a state into which people can fall at any time—a kind of constant threat to the stability and justice of human society.[11]

This constant threat is to be overcome, first of all, through the establishment of clear guidance—by the provision of a standard or criterion which will indicate to humanity what is the straight path. Such a criterion is given in the first place in the Qur'an, the book of God. In this book, given miraculously to Muhammad the Prophet, the judgments of God are made known and guidance is given to humanity.

All this again is standard Islamic teaching. What is interesting in the light of Mr. Barudi's points, however, is (again) the special emphasis given to revealed guidance in Wahhabi doctrine. There is the statement of the Saudi representative on Article 1 of the Declaration, which posits as a ground of human rights the notion that all human beings are endowed with reason and conscience. According to Mr. Barudi, this was not, and had never been, true. According to Wahhabi doctrine, "anybody who makes a judgment other than by the book of God is a *kafir*."[12]

Implicit in this statement is the notion that judgments of value find their only basis in the will of God, declared in revealed texts. Thus Wahhabi doctrine contains nothing of the notion of natural law or a nonrevelational knowledge of good and evil available to all human beings. According to Henri Laoust, Wahhabi teaching on such issues bears the imprint of Ash'ari doctrine, despite the criticisms of that doctrine by the school. Thus, justice must be understood with reference to God's will and action, which is the sole principle of good and evil. Things ordinary reason would indicate are right or just can be so only if God commands them; they might be reversed, if God willed. For example, lying is wrong only because God forbids it. The Lord of the worlds might have ordained lying, and if he were to do so, saying "lying is right," then "none could gainsay Him."[13]

3. The conclusion of all this is that a legitimate state must be organized along religious lines. Power, which is the main prerequisite for leadership of the Islamic community, is to be exercised in a struggle to disseminate true guidance and thus to overcome the threat of ignorance. To this end the leader of the Islamic community is to develop educational programs and to limit

corruption in government. He is to provide support for the scholars of Islam, who teach the people and advise the leader on the particulars of Islamic teaching. He is also to "wield the sword for good," in effect constraining forgetful and ignorant humanity in its own interests.[14]

In terms of religious liberty, these three emphases of Wahhabi teaching lead to notions that are strongly uniformist, à la John Cotton (see chapter 1). That is, given the view that the human condition largely consists in a lack of knowledge of the good, and given the perception that this lack was especially prevalent in the Arabian Peninsula prior to the advent of Wahhabi-Saudi cooperation, religion and the state need one another. Religion needs the support of state power for its spread and maintenance, and the state needs religion to guide the use of its power and provide a "social cement." To understand the correlation of Mr. Barudi's statements with Wahhabi teaching, one should recall his worry over the right to change one's religion. There are religious and political interests at stake in his opposition to the stipulation of such a "right," since turning from true guidance would indicate a return to ignorance and constitute a threat to social welfare.

Further, Wahhabi teaching (and Mr. Barudi's comments) reflects conservative and exclusivist tendencies that lend strong support to conformist social arrangements. Conservative tendencies, for example, appear in what Fazlur Rahman has called a noncritical acceptance of the past.[15] The Wahhabi movement identifies itself with the figure of Ahmad ibn Hanbal, a ninth-century scholar who asserted the priority of revealed texts in matters of faith and practice. With Ahmad, Wahhabi doctrine holds to the importance of the Qur'an (see above) and of texts (*hadith* reports) that tell of the exemplary practice (*sunna*) of the Prophet. Moreover, given that the collection of *hadith* reports like that of Ahmad took place some two hundred years after the death of Muhammad, there is a tendency to revere not only prophetic *sunna* but the people reporting on it. Thus, there is a *hadith* that cites a saying of Muhammad giving special authority to the first three generations of Muslims. Beyond this period Wahhabi teaching indicates that the consensus of Muhammad's community is not to be regarded as authoritative; it is rather to be evaluated on the basis of the Qur'an and those *hadith* reports that can be traced to the Prophet through exemplary figures of the early period.[16]

However, it seems that such notions, which are suggestive of the possibility of reform based on fresh interpretations of revealed texts, come to little in Wahhabi teaching. Laoust indicates that statements apparently justifying *ijtihad,* the principle of independent judgment based on revealed sources, are really insignificant in the Wahhabi system. While simple acceptance of the judgments of previous generations is forbidden in theory, the Wahhabis actually taught that even expert scholars are obligated to follow the important teachers of the Hanbali school.

In effect, the independent judgment advocated by Wahhabi teaching appears to involve a criticism of practices and beliefs that Hanbali scholars regarded as non-Islamic, even though they might be acceptable to other schools within Sunni Islam. Thus, the tendency toward exclusivism, expressed in the idea (and practice) of a holy struggle against such practices as praying at the tomb of an exemplary individual (a common practice among Muslims making the pilgrimage to Mecca), or against bedouin tribes resisting the idea that taxes should be paid to the Saudi regime as the representative of true Islam. In her exemplary study of *The Cohesion of Saudi Arabia*, Christine Moss Helms puts it well: "Any Muslim who, for whatever reason, fell into conflict with their [Wahhabis'] interpretation of Islam or challenged their authority was generally considered to be a *kafir* or *murtadd*, and was liable to the severest sanctions, although these were not clearly defined."[17] Ms. Helms reports that from 1910 to 1930, the period when the Saudi state began to take its modern shape, the Wahhabi-Saudi forces conquered large areas of the Arabian Peninsula, demanding payments of *zakat* (alms-tax) as a seal of allegiance to their alliance. She notes: "Those refusing *zakat* payment were liable to *jihad* despite the fact that in many cases they were Sunni Muslims." Exclusivist tendencies in Wahhabi doctrine, which amount to a claim that true guidance, that guidance given in revealed texts, is preserved in its pure form only within the Wahhabi school, thus appear to be demonstrated by Saudi practice in the early twentieth century.

Such tendencies also correspond to the resistance of Mr. Barudi to Article 18 of the Universal Declaration of Human Rights. At least, this seems a reasonable conclusion, given the evidence presented here. It appears that the Saudi representative was expressing ideas connected with the self perception of his nation as one born out of strenuous efforts to create an Islamic people in an environment characterized by ignorance and social strife. Its special mission, and the theological underpinnings thereof, support the foundation of a religious state, in which rights connected with religious liberty (as understood in the Declaration) are a threat to social stability and human welfare.

Islam and Pakistan

If al-Barudi's comments were the only expression of Islamic opinion on Article 18, or if Saudi Arabia were the only nation claiming an Islamic basis for its social arrangement, then our dialogue on religious liberty might well end here. Or at least it would be clear that such a dialogue could only take place on limited terms, such as the status of non-Islamic communities in an Islamic state, or other issues connected with the establishment of a state religion. In other words, the focus of discussion would be on the extent of religious *toleration,* rather than of religious liberty as intended in the Declaration.

To agree to such limitations would be premature at this point, however. That is so, if for no other reason, because of the statements of Zafrullah Khan on the agreement of Islam with the provisions of Article 18. He pointed out that the Qur'an states that "neither faith, nor conscience which gave birth to it, could have an obligatory character. The Koran expressly said: 'Let he who chooses to believe, believe, and he chooses to disbelieve, disbelieve,' and it formally condemned not lack of faith but hypocrisy." Further, the Pakistani delegation "considered that the essential point was to repeat that for its part the Moslem religion had unequivocally proclaimed the right to freedom of conscience and had declared itself against any kind of compulsion in matters of faith or religious practice."[18]

The disagreement with Mr. Barudi's response to Article 18, and perhaps the desire to identify Islam as something other than the religious and social pattern developed in Wahhabi-Saudi Arabia, evidenced here calls for further inquiry. In an attempt to understand Zafrullah Khan's position it is necessary to consider certain aspects of Indian (and Pakistani) Islam that will demonstrate the bases of Islamic disagreement at the United Nations in terms of unity and diversity in this world faith.

We may begin by investigating something of the intellectual context of Zafrullah Khan's comments. Again, the stress on ideas involves a conscious choice to focus on the religious heritage underlying the foreign minister's comments, rather than on factors inherent in Pakistan's political situation during the 1948 discussions.

In exploring Zafrullah Khan's remarks, it is interesting to note that he himself was an adherent of the movement known as Ahmadiyyat. Generally regarded as sectarian within the Islamic community, and more recently classified as non-Islamic under Pakistani law, this group holds to the view that the true meaning of the Qur'an has been obscured through the centuries, and has only recently (late nineteenth century) been restated by Mirza Ghulam Ahmad. According to Zafrullah Khan's own testimony, the true Qur'anic religion (as taught by Mirza Ghulam Ahmad) is one which enters into dialogue with other faiths and makes its appeal to the conscience of humanity, relying solely on persuasion.[19] While his attachment to the teaching of this group is interesting in connection with his own enthusiasm for Article 18 of the Declaration, it could hardly be taken as the foundation for a policy statement by the government of Pakistan. Ahmadiyyat has never enjoyed a real acceptance among the Muslims of Pakistan; the new Muslim state must have had other reasons in support of the foreign minister's comments for him to speak so boldly at the United Nations.

The more logical context for these comments would seem to be the attitude exemplified by Muhammad Ali Jinnah, the "Great Leader" of Pakistan, in his presidential address to the Constituent Assembly of Pakistan on 11 August 1947.[20] Speaking on the occasion of that Assembly's first meeting, and only a few days before the official birth of Pakistan, the president of the new state spoke about the problems its people would face and the kind of cooperation necessary to achieve success. Those interested in the well-being of Pakistan, he said, should concentrate on the welfare of its people, particularly the poor. They should begin to work together, forgetting past differences—even to the point of disregarding religious distinctions in the realm of politics:

If you change your past and work together in a spirit that every one of you, no matter to what community he belongs, no matter what relations he had with you in the past, no matter what is his colour, caste or creed, is first, second and last a citizen of this State with equal rights, privileges and obligations, there will be no end to the progress you will make.

I cannot emphasize it too much. We should begin to work in that spirit and in course of time all these angularities of the majority and minority communities, the Hindu community and the Muslim community—because even as regards Muslims you have Pathans, Punjabis, Shias, Sunnis and so on . . . will vanish.

To my mind, this problem of religious differences has been the greatest hindrance in the progress of India. Therefore, we must learn a lesson from this. You are free; you are free to go to your temples, you are free to go to your mosques or to any other places of worship in this State of Pakistan. You may belong to any religion or caste or creed—that has nothing to do with the business of the State.

Jinnah went on to speak of the parallels between Pakistan and the position of the English people prior to the achievement of toleration between Protestants and Catholics. He observed that

today, you might say with justice that Roman Catholics and Protestants do not exist; what exists now is that every man is a citizen, an equal citizen of Great Britain and they are all members of the Nation.

Now, I think we should keep that in front of us as an ideal and you will find that in course of time Hindus would cease to be Hindus and Muslims would cease to be Muslims, not in the religious sense, because that is the personal faith of each individual, but in the political sense as citizens of the state.

The resonance of Jinnah's statements with Article 18 of the Universal Declaration seems obvious.

What is less obvious is the Islamic status of Jinnah's comments. Indeed, given all that was involved in the campaign for a Muslim state in the Indian subcontinent, and given the strength of communal feelings on which Jinnah relied to bring Pakistan into being, one might well wonder, with a recent biographer, "What was he talking about? Had he simply forgotten where he was?" by calling communal loyalties into question.[21] In terms of the circumstances of Jinnah's life and career, it is tempting to view such "disjointed ramblings," as Wolpert describes the above remarks, as the result of his declining powers of concentration and discernment in connection with the illness that would take his life in 1948. Or at least one might say that Jinnah's single-minded devotion to the creation of Pakistan in the late 1930s and early 1940s had not given much time for thinking about the sort of state Pakistan, as a nation founded by and for the Muslim community in the subcontinent, might be. Given this lack Jinnah—trained as a British barrister and inspired by the liberalism of the Labour Party—simply asserted himself by calling on British history as an example for the new Muslim state.

What the precise role of Islam might have been in Jinnah's case is difficult to determine. It seems true that he was above all a political animal; and his position on Hindu-Muslim relations at any given period in his life seems to have been governed by political assessments, related to his position as not only a member and representative of Muslim (and therefore minority) interests, but as a Shi'a (and therefore a member of the "minority within the minority"). At the same time, it is possibly significant that Shi'ism, particularly the Twelver variety adopted by Jinnah as a young adult, contains notions of natural law and conscience which resonate with portions of the Western libertarian tradition. Thus Jinnah's liberalism might be as much a function of his religious convictions as vice versa.[22]

Whatever the case for Jinnah's status as a religious thinker, it is certainly true that his statements in the 11 August speech, as well as Zafrullah Khan's comments at the United nations, would have been in accord with certain tendencies in Indo-Pakistani Islam at the time. Overall, these tendencies involved the stipulation that Islam is relevant to and consonant with a modern (i.e., liberal) society; and that its relevance and consonance to and with this society is best indicated by the Qur'anic revelation. At times such "modernism" seems predicated on a (rather uncritical) assessment of Islam, as well as of modern society; at other times it appears to have asserted the necessity of rethinking the meaning of Islam on the basis of a fresh interpretation of the Qur'an.

The tendency to identify the tradition of Islam with the values and arrangements of modern, liberal society can be seen in such popular works as Amir 'Ali's *Spirit of Islam*. First published in 1891, the book went through numerous editions; it presented a version of Islam which emphasized its role in lifting the religious and moral consciousness of humanity to new (and essentially liberal) heights. Islam, it was said, established for the conscience of humanity a new concern for the welfare of women and a principle of equality that undermined permanent slavery. Its Prophet spoke against superstition and ignoble pursuits, and was thus on the side of those who advocate education and culture. Further, on the issues of concern to us here:

> By the laws of Islam, liberty of conscience and freedom of worship were allowed and guaranteed to the followers of every other creed under Moslem dominion. The passage in the Koran, "Let there be no compulsion in religion," testifies to the principles of toleration and charity inculcated by Islam. "If thy Lord had pleased, verily all who are in the world would have believed together." "Wilt thou then force men to believe when belief can come only from God?"
>
> "Adhere to those who forsake you; speak truth to your own heart; do good to every one that does ill to you": these are the precepts of a Teacher who has been accused of fanaticism and intolerance. Let it be remembered that these are the utterances, not of a powerless enthusiast or philosophical dreamer paralysed by the weight of opposing forces. These are the utterances of a man in the plenitude of his power, of the head of a sufficiently strong and well-organised State, able to enforce his doctrines with the edge of his reputed sword.[23]

With these remarks Amir 'Ali wished to show his readers—European Christians as well as Indian Muslims—that the spirit and force of Muhammad's life and teaching were one with that of liberal society.

The influence of *The Spirit of Islam*, according to Wilfred Cantwell Smith, was not so great in terms of its direct readership among Indian Muslims.[24] However, Smith considers the book to be important as representative of the thinking of a large group of Muslims earlier in this century, particularly the middle class. Here it is cited to illustrate the attitude, which Jinnah and others in his circle seem to have shared, that there is nothing about Islam that is inimical to values of individual freedom or institutions of religious liberty. Indeed, according to Zafrullah Khan's testimony, Islam provides a foundation for such values and institutions. That is, of course, Islam when it is rightly understood. Zafrullah Khan's Ahmadiyyat convictions provided him person-ally with the notion that a fresh interpretation of the Qur'an was needed, in order to meet the needs of twentieth-century humanity and in order to sweep away the dead weight of tradition. That much has been indicated.

It is also true, however, that this emphasis on rethinking Islam through a kind of "Protestant principle" of evaluating historical understandings of that faith in the light of the Qur'an had a wider place in Indian Islam than the fate of Ahmadiyyat might indicate. Thus, Sayyid Ahmad Khan (1817–98) devel-oped a critique of traditional Islam that emphasized the authority and clarity of the Qur'an and posited the right of every Muslim to judge God's will independent of the rulings of religious specialists and their emphasis on prec-edent. Motivated by a sense that Islam's potential for modern humanity lay in a reassertion of a rationality which had been obscured by tradition, Ahmad Khan proceeded from this starting point to argue that the rulings of previous generations on such issues as the justification of war, polygamy, and slavery should be overturned. In asserting and practicing the principle of independent judgment (*ijtihad*) in a way which the Wahhabi movement did not, Ahmad Khan demonstrated a way in which libertarian conceptions might be devel-oped within a tradition that was historically uniformist. That is, one might assert the priority of Qur'anic verses emphasizing freedom of conscience over the traditionally authoritative judgments of religious specialists.[25]

Similarly, and closer to the foundation of Pakistan, the discussion of Mu-hammad Iqbal (1877–1938) in *The Reconstruction of Religious Thought in Islam* argues that independent judgment (*ijtihad*) is the principle of move-ment in Islam.[26] It is that notion, or rule of discerning God's will, which allows Islam to develop its basic and universal message in relation to particu-lar social and historical contexts. The limitation that tradition placed on this principle in the interest of emphasizing the nonrelative nature of Islamic truth must be judged as contrary to the spirit of Islam, and ought to be done away with.

Following from this point, Iqbal argued that Turkey, as the first modernist nation among those traditionally connected with Islam, should be com-mended for facing the real question of modern Muslims—whatever the merits of its particular reforms of historic Islam. That question, simply stated, is "whether or not the Law of Islam is capable of evolution." According to Iqbal, the answer is yes, and the issue should be faced in the spirit of 'Umar, second caliph after the Prophet. When faced with the death of the Prophet, 'Umar "had the moral courage to utter these remarkable words: 'The Book of God is sufficient for us.' "[27]

Thus, in Iqbal's influential treatise, the Qur'an becomes the primary source of Muslim judgments, with *hadith* reports representing a source of traditional wisdom for the application of Qur'anic principles more than an authority in themselves. And even the Qur'an, while primary in the development of practical judgments by Muslims, is not the definitive source of law and ethics that Wahhabi teaching seems to argue for. For Iqbal, the Qur'an's first purpose is not the provision of legal precedents, but the awakening in human beings of a higher consciousness of their relation to God and the universe. It is a book, then, that is capable of multiple interpretations by those whose consciousness of this relation it awakens, according to their social and historical position. As Iqbal had it: "The teaching of the Qur'an that life is a process of progressive creation necessitates that each generation, guided yet unhampered by the work of its predecessor, should be permitted to solve its own problems."[28]

There is a great deal more to Muhammad Iqbal and Ahmad Khan as religious thinkers than can be indicated here. Iqbal's doctrine of the self, for example, in particular his understanding of the ways in which the self attains the knowledge of God, is quite interesting, and with its connections to the Sufi aspect of the tradition of Islam has its own implications for religious liberty.

It is difficult to say, though, whether or not these aspects of Iqbal's thought contributed in any substantive way to the sense, exemplified in the remarks of Zafrullah Khan and evidently felt by an influential segment of those involved in the founding of Pakistan, that it was possible to approve Article 18 of the Universal Declaration of Human Rights on Islamic grounds. What seems clear is rather that the tendencies of modernism to assert (or assume) the basic affinity between Islam and liberal patterns of social organization, and to do so (at times) on the basis of a critical assessment of Islamic history or tradition via a fresh interpretation of the Qur'an, were fairly common in Indo-Pakistani Islam. Indeed, as is plain in Zafrullah Khan's statement, it was the libertarian tendencies of the Qur'an which impressed him, and which provided the Islamic grounds for his support of Article 18.

Islamic Disagreement: Problems and Possibilities

The evidence presented thus far seems quite clearly to point to both unity and diversity in the tradition of Islam; a unity and diversity which make it possible to speak of Islamic disagreement—disagreement, that is, which is nonetheless Islamic in that the parties agree on certain fundamentals. In this case the main agreement is on the special place of the Qur'an in human (and Islamic) history as a text in which God speaks to humanity. That such agreement would exist seems almost too obvious to state; Islam is nothing if not a way of understanding what it means to be human or live well in terms of a response to the Qur'anic event.

Nevertheless, it seems necessary to state this fundamental unity in view of the equally obvious disagreement between Islamic representatives at the United Nations and in view of certain developments in the Islamic world that are nearer in time to the present study. Thus, while the Wahhabi doctrines that correlate so well with al-Barudi's statements on Article 18 reflect the acceptance of certain historic or traditional interpretations of the Qur'an as authoritative (i.e., those of the Hanbali school), "Modernist" Islam in the Indian context expresses the idea that fresh interpretations of the Qur'an are necessary to every generation, even if they conflict with venerable precedents. Similarly, Wahhabi teaching appears as exclusivist, positing a radical break between things Islamic and non-Islamic, the latter being expressions of the time or state of ignorance (*jahiliyya*) and thus a threat to the security and well-being of humanity. Given the way in which a noncritical attitude toward the past seems a part of the Wahhabi system, such exclusivism expresses itself in a fundamental conservatism, even traditionalism, which finds it difficult to absorb modern (liberal) notions of social organization—religious liberty, for example.

Indian modernism, on the other hand, supposes that there is no conflict between Islam and modern, liberal society. That is, there is no conflict between the two properly understood. In Ahmad Khan and Muhammad Iqbal one finds the notion that true Islam involves a return to the Qur'an as Islam's primary text; in the former, and in Amir 'Ali's *Spirit of Islam,* one finds in addition the idea that this true Islam contains nothing inimical to liberal society. Indeed, Amir 'Ali seems to tell us that true Islam is the best foundation for such a society, other faiths either expressing lower points in the religious evolution of humankind or being made less useful through the errors of their adherents. Both these attitudes seem to have been present among Muslim leaders at the foundation of Pakistan. Both seem to lie behind Zafulllah Khan's speech at the United Nations.

The bases of disagreement, then, appear to lie in the Qur'anic text and the way in which it is to be interpreted by and for the Muslim community, just as the unity that makes it reasonable to speak of the disagreeing parties as Islamic exists in an acknowledgment of the Qur'an as a unique and authoritative text. Once this is said, there appear problems and possibilities for a dialogue between representatives of Islamic and Western cultures on the subject of religious liberty. The central problem may be stated as follows: Is there one way of responding to the Qur'an that is more "Islamic" than others? In the case presented here, in particular, it is appropriate to ask how Islamic the modernist approach is, or was. This is so because recent developments in the Islamic world, usually described in terms of a resurgence of Islamic values, sometimes appear to share more with the Wahhabi understanding of Islam than with Indian modernism. This is so particularly in terms of the relation between Islamic and Western-liberal patterns of social organization. In the Pakistani context, for example, the influence of Abu'l-A'la Mawdudi's Islamic Party (*Jama'at-e Islami*), while in certain respects very different from that of Wahhabism, nevertheless shows the same tendencies to reject liberal notions of natural law and liberty of conscience as the latter.[29] It is indeed one of the ironies of Pakistani history that in the 1950s the foreign minister who had spoken so positively of the agreement between Islam and Article 18's provisions for religious liberty would find his position in the cabinet threatened by the fact that the Islamic Party and others regarded him as a heretic (for his association with Ahmadiyyat.) More recently, as mentioned, Ahmadiyyat was classified by the Pakistani government as a non-Islamic sect, to be governed under rules pertaining to minority communities. Such developments reflect, not the religious liberty intended by Article 18, but more traditional patterns of religious toleration.

It is difficult to adjudicate the issues suggested by such developments, and indeed by the question stated above: Is there one way of responding to the Qur'an that is more "Islamic" than others? In a sense, what is called for is a definition of orthodox Islam—the achievement of which is extremely difficult, since there does not seem to be any agreed-upon mechanism for the Muslim community to establish it.[30] The most that could be suggested, given the evidence presented thus far, is that orthodox Islam involves the conception that being human or living well involves response to the Qur'an. That is certainly a minimal definition, but it provides a certain framework by which one might begin to deal with the question of how Islamic the modernist approach might be. That is, it is sometimes argued that modernism with its notions of rethinking tradition and its acceptance of liberal patterns of social organization is or was more a function of Western influence than Islamic. Jinnah, Zafrullah Khan, and others are thus viewed as reflecting tendencies that are non-Islamic, having little and perhaps no basis in Islamic sources.

Our discussion thus far leaves this open. What it suggests is that for our dialogue on religious liberty to proceed further, we must probe more deeply into the meaning of the Qur'anic text. More than that, we must attend to certain ways of interpreting the Qur'an relative to religious liberty, ways which Muslims consider to be significant or authoritative. Thus, the next portion of our discussion deals with certain problems related to religious liberty in the light of the Qur'an and portions of the *tafsir*, of exegetical literature produced by the Muslim community. Having explored that literature, perhaps we will be in a better position to know what the Islamic basis for religious liberty might or might not be.

NOTES

1. Adda B. Bozeman, *The Future of Law in a Multicultural World* (Princeton: Princeton University Press, 1971), 76.

2. See Max Stackhouse, *Creeds, Society, and Human Rights* (Grand Rapids: Eerdmans, 1984). On p. 40 Stackhouse advances a brief comment on Islam which is taken further in two essays : "Democracy and the World's Religions," *This World* (1982): 108-20; and "Theology, History and Human Rights," *Soundings* 67 (1984); 191-208.

3. James P. Piscatori, "Human Rights in Islamic Political Culture," *Moral Imperatives of Human Rights,* ed. Kenneth W. Thompson (Washington: University Press of America, 1980), 157-58, 144.

4. This focus on Islamic contributions to UN discussion was suggested by Piscatori's article. My criticism of his essay is simply that he fails to take into account the Pakistani assessment of Article 18, and thus reaches conclusions that are one-sided.

5. Joseph Lash gives an interesting account of Mrs. Roosevelt's campaign for the Declaration in *Eleanor: The Years Alone* (New York: Norton, 1972). The only complete account of the discussion is the *Official Records* of the UN General Assembly; see esp. those pertaining to the 3rd session, 1948-49, 3rd Committee, Pt. 2; and 3rd session, 1948-49, Plenary Meetings.

6. *Official Records,* 3rd session, 1948-49, 3rd Committee, Pt. 2, p. 49.

7. *Official Records,* 3rd session, 3rd Committee, 120. I will refer to the various articles of the Declaration as numbered in the final version. During the committee and plenary discussions various drafts gave a different ordering: our Article 18 was at one point 16, at another 19.

8. *Official Records,* 3rd session, Plenary Meeting, 889-91.

9. Cited in Christine Moss Helms, *The Cohesion of Saudi Arabia* (Baltimore: Johns Hopkins University Press, 1965), and H. St. J. Philby, *Arabia of the Wahhabis* (London: Frank Cass, 1977). On Wahhabi doctrine see Henri Laoust, *Essai sur les doctrines sociales et politiques de Taki-d-Din Ahmad b. Taimiya* (Cairo: L'Institut Francais d' Archeologie Orientale, 1939), 2:506-40, and Appendix, "Le foi des Wahhabites."

10. Helms, *Cohesion,* 83-84.

11. This characteristic of *jahiliyya* is pointed out by T. Izutsu in his *God and Man in the Koran* (Tokyo: Keio Institute of Cultural and Linguistic Studies, 1964). Note also its use in contemporary Islamic thought, esp. political writing—e.g., in Hasan al-Banna or Sayyid Qutb.

12. Helms, *Cohesion,* 85.

13. On al-Ash'ari's ethics, see John Kelsay, "Religion and Morality in Islam: A Proposal Concerning Islamic Ethics in the Formative Period" (Ph.D. diss., University of Virginia, 1985) and literature cited there.

14. See Laoust, *Essai;* also W. Madelung, "Imama," *Encyclopedia of Islam,* ed. Gibb and Kramers.

15. See Fazlur Rahman, *Islam,* 2nd ed. (Chicago: University of Chicago Press, 1979); also *Islam and Modernity* (University of Chicago Press, 1982). Of course, Rahman means here the past represented in the consensus of the early Muslims.

16. On Ahmad ibn Hanbal and other subjects connected with the early development of Islam see W. Montgomery Watt, *The Formative Period of Islamic Thought* (Edinburgh: University of Edinburgh Press, 1973); also Marshal G. S. Hodgson, *The Venture of Islam* (Chicago: University of Chicago Press, 1974), vol. 1. Similarly, George Makdisi, "Hanbalite Islam," *Studies in Islam,* ed. and trans. Merlin L. Swartz (Oxford: Oxford University Press, 1981).

17. Helms, *Cohesion,* 97.

18. *Op cit. Official Records,* 3rd session, 3rd Committee, p. 120.

19. See Mohammed Zafrullah Khan, *The Message of Ahmadiyyat* (India: Nazir Dawat-o-Tablish, 1970); also Freeland Abbott, *Islam and Pakistan* (Ithaca: Cornell University Press, 1968).

20. The text is published in *Speeches and Writings of Mr. Jinnah,* collected and ed. Jamil-ud-Din Ahmad (Lahore: Sh. Muhammad Ashraf, 1964), 2:399–405.

21. Stanley Wolpert, *Jinnah of Pakistan* (New York: Oxford University Press, 1984), 340. See also Hector Bolitho, *Jinnah: Creator of Pakistan* (London: John Murray, 1964).

22. Wolpert's study sheds very little light here, and what there is seems contradictory. For example, on p. 18 he indicates that "religion never played an important role in Jinnah's life—except for its political significance." Yet, in the same sentence, "he left the Aga Khan's 'Sevener' Khoja community at this stage of his maturation [in his late twenties], opting instead to join the less hierarchically structured Isna' Ashari sect of 'Twelver' Khojas, who acknowledged no leader." Wolpert implies this shift had to do with the Twelver connections of Jinnah's friend Justice Badruddin Tyabji (1844–1906), whose commitments, as publicly articulated, had to do with "secular liberal" modernism. It is my understanding that Tyabji was actually an Ismaili of the Fatimid branch. More important than this bit of information, however, is the following issue. Given the picture supplied by David Little (above) of the connections between Christian theology and a branch of that ideology usually understood as secular, liberal, and modernist, one wonders if a Muslim community emphasizing some similar themes (natural law, etc.) might not have enabled a Justice Tyabji, or a Jinnah, to feel that their affinity with liberalism had religious legitimacy. One suspects that the interplay of religious and political feeling may be more complex than Wolpert shows, though it is difficult to know, at this point. On Twelver Shi'ism and its theological position, see Abdulaziz Sachedina, *Islamic Messianism* (Albany: State University of New York Press, 1981). Ayesha Jalal, *The Sole Spokesman* (Cambridge: Cambridge University Press, 1985), provides a somewhat fuller treatment of Jinnah in relation to certain religious trends. For example, she notes the response of Jinnah to Muhammad Iqbal's 1937 suggestion that the Muslim League enact a socioeconomic program based on the "Law of Islam." Jinnah was "too shrewd and too secular to change this particular hare." Again, the (1943–44) call of certain Muslim Leaguers from Punjab to make Pakistan an Islamic state was dealt with by Jinnah's statement: "'the Constitution and the Government . . . will be what the people decide' . . . By inference, every Muslim had the right to try his hand at shaping the future by

Islam and Religious Liberty

convincing his co-religionists" (pp. 95–96). As Jalal indicates, Jinnah's hope was for a secular, pluralistic society (p. 122). Nevertheless, she does not explore the question with which I am concerned here: viz., did Jinnah conceive his secular political vision as having an Islamic basis?

23. Syed Ameer Ali, *The Spirit of Islam* (London: Methuen, 1967), 212.

24. Wilfred Cantwell Smith, *Modern Islam in India* (London: Gollonez, 1946) 51ff.

25. See Christian W. Troll, *Sayyid Ahmad Khan: A Reinterpretation of Muslim Theology* (New Delhi: Vikas Publishing House, 1978), which contains translations of a number of Ahmad's works, as well as an exemplary study of the development of his thought. Sheila McDonough, *Muslim Ethics and Modernity* (Waterloo: Wilfrid Laurier University Press, 1984) also contains a helpful study of certain aspects of Ahmad Khan's thought.

26. Muhammad Iqbal, *The Reconstruction of Religious Thought in Islam* (Lahore: Sh. Muhammad Ashraf, 1968), 146–80.

27. Iqbal, *Reconstruction,* p. 162.

28. Iqbal, *Reconstruction,* p. 168.

29. See Mawdudi, *Islamic Law and Constitution,* 2nd ed., trans. and ed. Khurshid Ahmad (Lahore: Islamic Publications, 1960); also McDonough, *Muslim Ethics.*

30. Aside from the relatively loose and in some ways uncertain legal principle of consensus. On this, see McDonough, *Muslim Ethics,* 105–06.

3. Freedom of Conscience and Religion in the Qur'an

This chapter will examine the verses of the Qur'an dealing with religious liberty in view of the issues raised by David Little in the opening chapter of this book. To do so is of singular importance, since Little's suggestion that there is greater affinity between Islam and the West on questions of freedom of conscience and religion than is usually thought is based on his reading of the Qur'an. In addition, when one turns to contemporary statements on these issues, one finds representatives of various Muslim communities appealing to the Qur'an in support of their positions. This fact, as discussed by John Kelsay, indicates the importance of the Qur'an for Muslim self understanding, as well as the need to clarify what the Qur'anic teaching on matters of freedom of conscience and religion might be. Accordingly, I shall explore the Western concept of conscience as it relates to the Qur'an, especially in terms of the ideas of guidance and coercion in matters of faith.

Preliminaries

Since this essay is concerned with the analytical examination of these concepts in the Qur'an, and since the Qur'an itself does not deal with these ideas directly or systematically, my attempt will involve two lines of inquiry: first, examination of Qur'anic exegetical material in order to discover what interpreters of the Islamic scripture have understood regarding the relevant concepts; second, analysis of these materials in the light of Little's essay, so as to show what constitutes tolerance or freedom of conscience and religion in Islamic revelation.[1]

It is important to state briefly my justification for following the first line of inquiry. In his essay "The Ethical Presuppositions of the Qur'an," George F. Hourani has ruled against using the classical Arabic exegesis of the Qur'an to determine the nature of its internal ethical concepts "essentially because they [classical exegetes] belonged to schools of theology or jurisprudence which had taken up positions on the question at issue—often for complex historical reasons arising subsequently to the Qur'an."[2] At the same time, he acknowledges that the Qur'an "by its nature and purpose is not a theoretical book of theology and therefore takes up no explicit positions" on the related question of ethics.

Accordingly, Hourani admits that in order to study the Qur'an in this way, one must look for its assumptions. He proceeds to analyze ethical terms and sentences in the Qur'an, taking into account the historical and philological contexts as he understands them, and he concludes convincingly, though with due caution, that to some extent the "exercise of human ethical judgment independent of revelation is permitted by the Qur'an, but no precision emerges about the extent." Thus Hourani leaves little doubt that historical and philological considerations are necessary for understanding the Qur'an in its own terms.

These considerations suggest the need for a meticulous sifting of the exegetical materials dealing with the Qur'an, both classical and contemporary, in order to bring to light the various (and subtle) possibilities of interpretation. After all, the classical commentaries were produced by well-trained philologists and historians who, although they were committed to one theological position, frequently discussed their opponents' expositions at length before offering an alternative of their own. By weighing their arguments, very much as we do those of more modern exegetes such as Hourani, A. J. Arbery, or Fazlur Rahman,[3] we may hope to come a little closer to a fair interpretation of the ethical terms and passages in the Qur'an. My primary task, therefore, will be to analyze ethicoreligious concepts relevant to the subject of freedom of conscience and religion on the basis of Islamic exegetical literature, and then to formulate an account of the structure and content of these concepts in Islam. The investigation of this literature, which was produced by different schools of Islamic theology and ethics, will involve an analysis of the terms each group used to express its beliefs and assumptions regarding the notion of conscientious commitment in Islam. This investigation, it is hoped, will demonstrate the reasons for the deep tension in Islamic experience between a tolerant, pluralistic spirit, on the one hand, and a more regimented, exclusivist stance on the other.

Freedom of Conscience and Religion in the Qu'ran

As background to the discussion of the concept of conscience in the Qur'an, it is relevant first to identify briefly some major types of exegetical literature. From the early days of Islam attention was paid to the interpretation of the sacred text. Moreover, every close associate of the Prophet participated in this intellectual activity, since every listener had to interpret the revealed text for himself. During the lifetime of the Prophet some of the problems related to the comprehension of the Qur'an were referred to him, and he elaborated the revelation by giving explanations regarding the proper context and application of individual portions of it. These statements by the Prophet were incorporated in early exegesis.

On the basis of the information given in Muslim exegetical works, it is possible to discern three basic approaches to Qur'anic interpretation: (1) traditional (largely using the exegetical traditions of the early community to explicate the "occasions of revelation" of the text); (2) theological (expounding theological viewpoints held by the proponents of various schools through the Qur'anic interpretation); and (3) mystical (interpreting through extensive allegorization of the Qur'anic language, in order to apprehend the inner meaning of the text).[4] The works I have consulted for the present study are largely theological and traditional, since they yield the most relevant materials.

Theological exegesis of the Qur'anic material was dominated by the proponents of the two major schools of dialectical theology: the Mu'tazilite and the Ash'arite. It was in the works of these two schools that questions of ethical knowledge were treated in detail from the viewpoint of conflicting ethical theories. Since the question of the nature of good and evil is directly relevant to our discussion about conscience and guidance, it is worthwhile to describe at the outset the two respective theories.

The Mu'tazilite approach to Qur'anic interpretation is based on a metaphorical interpretation of the text to support certain dogmatic presuppositions and conclusions. The basic Mu'tazilite thesis is that human beings, as free agents, are responsible before a just God. Furthermore, good and evil are rational categories which can be known through reason, independently of revelation. God created man's intellect in such a way that it is capable of perceiving good and evil objectively. This is the corollary of the main thesis, for God's justice depends on the objective knowledge of good and evil as determined by reason, whether the Lawgiver pronounces it so or not. In other words, the Mu'tazilites asserted the efficacy of natural reason as a source of spiritual and ethical knowledge, maintaining, to use Hourani's classification, a form of rationalist objectivism.[5] The Mu'tazilite approach to

Qur'anic exegesis found its best exponent in Mahmud b. 'Umar al-Zamakhshari (d. 1144). His commentary has exercised great influence in the Sunni world, although his theological inferences have consistently been either opposed or rejected.

The Mu'tazilite standpoint was bound to be challenged. As Hourani has pointed out, the question of how extensive the Qur'anic allowance for independent reasoning in matters of value might be is a complex and difficult one. Thus, while the Qur'an admits some capacity for ethical knowledge independent of supernatural guidance, it is not surprising that the Ash'arites rejected the idea of natural reason as an autonomous source of ethical knowledge. They maintained that good and evil are as God decrees them to be, and that it is presumptuous to judge God on the basis of categories that God has provided for directing human life. For the Ash'arite there is no way, within the bounds of ordinary logic, to explain the relation of God's power to human actions. It is more realistic just to maintain that everything that happens is the result of his will, without explanation or justification. However, it is important to distinguish between the actions of a responsible human being and the motions attributed to natural laws. Human responsibility is not the result of free choice, a function which, according to the Mu'tazilites, determines the way an action is produced; rather, God alone creates all actions directly, but in some actions a special quality of "voluntary acquisition" is superimposed by God's will that makes the individual a voluntary agent and responsible. Consequently, human responsibility is the result of the divine will known through revealed guidance. Values have no foundation but the will of God that imposes them. This attitude of the Ash'arites to ethical knowledge, according to Hourani's classification, would be known as theistic subjectivism. That means that ethical values are dependent upon the determinations of the will of God expressed in the form of revelation, which is both eternal and immutable. This approach found its leading exponent in Fakhr al-Din al-Razi (d. 1209). His commentary marks the consummation of Ash'arite exegesis and includes material from all possible areas of Islamic scholarship to support the Ash'arite thesis regarding divine omnipotence.[6]

We may now proceed to the discussion of the concept of conscience in the Qur'an. This can best be treated within a general discussion of guidance in Islamic revelation, since the Qur'an does not provide us with a theoretical framework treating the categories of religious and ethical knowledge such as one might find, for instance, in works on systematic theology. Nevertheless, it is clear that there is a Qur'anic idea of conscience, connected to its over-

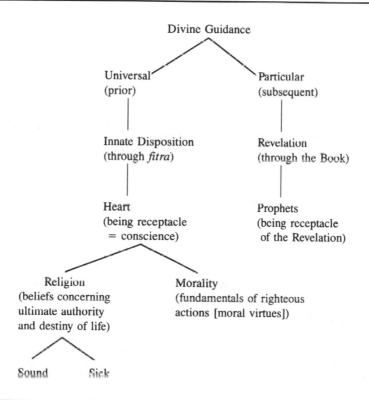

Figure 1.

whelming concern with the guidance of human beings to their ultimate goal. It is possible to schematize the general framework provided by the Qur'an as shown in Figure 1. The question of conscience in the Qur'an is connected with the idea of *fitra*, the innate disposition created by God as a necessary medium of universal guidance. As we shall see, there is a logical relationship between guidance and conscience, with the possibility of conscience being designated as sound or sick in accordance with one's voluntary acceptance or rejection of divine guidance. Furthermore, it will become clear that Little's discussion about conscience and its role in the idea of freedom of faith in the Western context is equally applicable to the Islamic context.

Islam and Religious Liberty

The Question of Guidance in the Qur'an

Guidance[7] in the Qur'an constitutes the way in which God's purpose in creating human beings is achieved.

> By the soul; and That which shaped it
> and inspired it to [know the
> difference between] lewdness and
> godfearing!
>> Prosperous is he who purifies it,
>> and failed has he who seduces it.
> (91:7-10)

In order for human beings to attain the purpose for which they are created, they need to be adequately guided. Thus God, according to this verse, has endowed human beings with the necessary cognition and volition to further their comprehension of the purpose for which they are created and to realize that purpose by using their knowledge. Moreover, the verse also makes it plain that the distinction between lewdness (evil) and godfearing (good) is ingrained in the soul in the form of inspiration, a form of guidance with which God has favored human beings. It is through this guidance that human beings are expected to develop the ability to judge their actions and to choose that which will lead them to prosperity. But this is not an easy task to achieve. It involves spiritual and moral development, something that is most challenging in the light of the basic human weaknesses indicated by the Qur'an:

> Surely man was created fretful,
> when evil visits him, impatient,
> when good visits him, grudging.
> (70:19-20)

These weaknesses reveal a basic tension that must be resolved by further acts of guidance by God. It is at this point that God sends the prophets and the books (revealed messages) to show human beings how to change their character and bring it in conformity with the divine plan for human conduct:

> That is the Book, wherein is no doubt,
> a guidance to the godfearing . . .
> Those who [rely] upon guidance from their Lord,
> those are ones who prosper. (2:2,5)

The guidance from God signifies the direction he provides to procure that which is desirable, first by creating in the soul a disposition that can guard against spiritual peril (if a person hearkens to its warnings), and then by further strengthening this natural guidance through the Book and the Prophet. Guidance in the sense of "showing the path" is a fundamental feature of the Qur'an and is reiterated throughout to emphasize the fact that this form of guidance is part of human nature; that is, it is universal and available to all who aspire to become godfearing and prosperous.

However, human beings can reject this guidance, although they cannot produce any valid excuse for the rejection. Of course, rejection pertains to the procuring or appropriating of that which is desirable, and not to the act of apprehending in the first place what is desirable. Thus when God denies guidance to those who do not believe in his revelations (19:104), the denial pertains to the procurement of the desirable end, and *not* to the initial guidance that is originally engraved upon the hearts of all human beings. "And [We] guided them on a straight path" (4:70) points to the guidance signifying the procurement of the good end. It implies that this guidance is available to an individual after that person has consented to lead a life of uprightness (*taqwa*). In another verse the Qur'an makes it even more explicit that this latter aspect of guidance makes it possible for a person to achieve that which is desirable:

Whomsoever God desires to guide,
He expands his breast to Islam [to submit himself to the will of God in order to
   procure the desirable goal];
whomsoever He desires to lead astray [because of the personal choice not to
   submit]
He makes his breast narrow, tight,
as if he were climbing to heaven.
So God lays [malediction]
upon those who believe not. (6:125)

It becomes evident, then, that the Qur'an is speaking about two forms of guidance. As a matter of fact, all the exegetes in their commentaries on verse 2:2, "That is the Book, wherein is no doubt, a guidance to the godfearing," distinguished the two forms in response to the question as to why the Book should be revealed as guidance to the godfearing, for they have presumably already attained guidance in order to become godfearing in the first place. The first form is the one by means of which an individual becomes godfearing (*muttaqi*), while the second is the one which God bestows *after* the attainment of piety or moral consciousness (*taqwa*). This latter guidance helps the individual to remain unshakable when encountering unbelievers and hypocrites. *Taqwa*, which is "keen spiritual and moral perception and motivation,"[8] is a comprehensive attribute that touches all aspects of faith when faith is put into practice.

However, human beings can reject faith, and that results in misguidance (*idlal*). It is important to note that the Qur'an considers misguidance or "leading astray" to be God's response to unsatisfactory actions or attitudes on the part of individuals who have chosen to reject the faith. As such, they deserve it:

> How shall God guide a people who have disbelieved after they believed? . . .
> God guides not the people of evildoers. (3:8)

> Surely those who disbelieve after they have believed
> and then increase in unbelief—their repentance
> shall not be accepted; those are the ones who stray. (3:90)

The above passage implies human responsibility for being led astray. Human beings are given the choice to accept or reject the faith, and they bear the consequences of their choice. However, the Qur'an also makes frequent references to the effect that

> they [the unbelievers] say, "What did God desire by this
> for a similitude?" Thereby He leads
> many astray, and thereby He guides
> many; and thereby He leads none astray
>   save the ungodly
> such as break the covenant of God. (2:26)

This verse imputes the responsibility of "leading astray" to God. The Muslim exegetes have correctly distinguished between two kinds of misguidance so as to explicate statements of this nature. The first kind of misguidance follows from the choice made by an individual. It causes corrupt attributes such as disbelief (*kufr*) and hypocrisy (*nifaq*), whereas the second kind of misguidance confirms these attributes in that person. This is the point of the following verse:

> In their heart is a sickness,
>   and God has increased their sickness,
> and there awaits them a painful chastisement
>   for that they have cried lies. (2:10)

The first kind of sickness is imputed to the person, implying a willful act which results in spiritual affliction, while the second stage of sickness is imputed to God, who caused their hearts to swerve when they swerved

Freedom of Conscience and Religion in the Qu'ran

(61:5). This means that God does not guide people who have neglected to respond to that universal guidance ingrained in the human soul (91:7), by means of which they could have helped themselves to understand their true role on earth.

From the above observations about guidance and misguidance it would be accurate to visualize people who possess *taqwa*—"keen spiritual and moral consciousness and motivation"—as being situated between universal guidance and revelational guidance. In other words, being equipped with the necessary cognition and volition, they are ready to follow the commands of God to attain prosperity. On the other hand, unbelievers and hypocrites can be visualized as being situated between the two forms of misguidance. By having allowed the heart to become "sick," they have allowed correct judgment and the sharp sense of personal responsibility which is theirs by nature to become dull.

Since the question of guidance is related to the question of the source of knowledge of ethical values in both classical and modern Qur'anic exegesis, I have taken some care to explicate these various forms of guidance in the Qur'an. Significantly, it is on this point that theological differences are rooted in conflicting conceptions of human responsibility. The Mu'tazilites, who emphasized the complete responsibility of human beings, upheld the concept of human free will in responding to the call of both natural guidance and guidance through revelation. On the other hand, the Ash'arites, who upheld the omnipotence of God, denied man any role in responding to divine guidance. As a matter of fact, according to them, it was impossible for an individual to accept or reject faith unless God willed it. In truth, the Qur'an contains a complex view of human responsibility. It allows for both human decision and divine omnipotence in the matter of guidance.[9]

Actually, the concept of universal guidance has wider implications than merely demonstrating the existence of volitional capacity in the human soul (91:7) and providing human responsibility in the development of a keen sense of spiritual and moral perception and motivation. It appears that the Qur'an regards humanity as having been one nation with reference to the universal guidance (the "prior" [*sabiqa*] guidance), before the particular guidance through revelation (the "subsequent" [*lahiqa*] guidance) was sent:

> The people were one nation; then God sent forth
> the Prophets, good tidings to bear
> and warning, and He sent down with them
> the Book with the truth, that He might
> decide between the people touching their differences. (2:213)

Islam and Religious Liberty

The universal guidance treats all human beings as equal and as potential believers in God before they become distinguished through the more particular guidance as believers, unbelievers, hypocrites, and so on.

On the basis of the notion of universal guidance, it is possible to speak of natural-moral grounds of human conduct in the Qur'an which parallel Paul's presuppositions in Romans 2:14–15 and 3:19. These passages seem to refer to an objective and universal moral nature on the basis of which all human beings are to be treated equally and held equally accountable to God. In other words, certain moral prescriptions follow from a common human nature and are regarded as independent of particular spiritual beliefs, even though all practical guidance ultimately springs from the same source, namely from God. It is significant to note that the term the Qur'an uses to designate goodness (moral virtue)—with which all human beings are exhorted to comply—is *al-ma'ruf,* meaning the well-known, generally recognized, and even universally accepted:

> Prescribed for you, when any of you
> is visited by death, and he leaves behind
> some goods, is to make testament
> in favor of his parents and kinsmen (in goodness, *al-ma'ruf*)
>   (i.e., in a generally recognized way)—an obligation
> on the godfearing [i.e., those who possess *taqwa*
> (spiritual and moral awareness)]. 2:180

"Goodness" in this passage is to be understood in the way the Arabs understood it conventionally, before the Qur'an was revealed to supplement the common ethical sense of *al-ma'ruf.*

It should be borne in mind that the Qur'an was revealed against the background of the tribal society of Arabia and that moral exhortations in the Qur'an were ultimately the outgrowth of their everyday meaning in the Arabic expressions. Thus, the notion of *'adl* (justice) in the Qur'an, as explained by Ibn Manzur, the author of a classical Arabic lexicon, is "the thing that is established in the mind as being straightforward."[10] Anything that is not upright or in order is regarded as *jawr* or unjust, unfair. The two literal meanings of *'adl*—namely, "straight" and "departure"—are implied in the conceptual sense of straightforwardness and uprightness. Needless to say, the notions of right and wrong are implied in the terms *'adl* and *jawr,* as these terms are often used in the broadest sense to include objective moral values. The objective nature of the concept of justice in the Qur'an is summarized in a letter written by an early jurist-theologian, Sa'id b. Jubayr, in reply to an

inquiry about the meaning of the term *'adl* by the caliph 'Abd al-Malik
(d. 705):

> *'Adl* [justice] may have four significations:
> [First,] justice in making decisions, in
> accordance with [the sense implied in] God's
> command [in the Qur'an]: ". . . and when you judge
> between the people, judge with justice" [4:61].
> [Second,] justice in speech, as construed in
> His command: ". . . and when you speak, be just"
> [6:153]; [third,] justice in [the pursuit of]
> the hereafter, as understood in His guidance:
> ". . . and beware a day when no soul for another
> shall give satisfaction, and no counterpoise
> (*'adl*) shall be accepted from it, nor any
> intercession shall be profitable to it" [2:117];
> [fourth,] justice in the sense of attributing
> an equal to God, as implied in His saying: ". . .
> the unbelievers ascribe equals (*ya'dilun*) to
> their Lord."
> As for the passage [where God says]: "You will
> not be able to be equitable (*ta'dilu*) between
> your wives, be you ever so eager" [4:128],
> 'Ubayda al-Salmani and al-Dahhaq are of the
> opinion that [men's inability to be equitable]
> meant [their inability to be so] in respect to
> love and intercourse. [Moreover, when someone
> says:] "So-and-so has done justice to so-and-so"
> it means that one is equitable to the other. . . .
> Justice in [the context of] weight and measurement
> means [that a certain object is] equal [to another]
> in weight or size. [If] you did justice between
> two things or you did justice between so-and-so
> and so-and-so, it means that you have made two things,
> or between one and another person, to be equal or
> the like of one another [respectively]. The doing of
> justice for a [certain] thing means to make it
> straight. It is said that justice means the rating
> of a thing as equal to a thing of another kind
> so as to make it like the latter.[11]

This explanation of the notion of justice with reference to the Qur'anic
passages where the notion occurs demonstrates an important point: that jus-

tice in revelation, which denotes moral virtues like fairness, balance, temperance, and straightforwardness, could not become intelligible without reference to an objective state of affairs. Indeed, the notion of divine justice logically appeals to those universally objective values "ingrained in the human soul" (91:8); in this way it becomes comprehensible. In an extremely important passage the Qur'an recognizes the universality and objective nature of moral virtue (goodness), a nature which transcends different religions and religious communities and admonishes humankind "to be forward in good work":

> To every one
> of you [religious communities] We have appointed (a law) and (a way of conduct).
> If God had willed, He would have made you
> one nation [on the basis of that law and that way]; but [He did not do so] that He
>   may try you
> in what has come to you. So be you forward [i.e., compete with one another]
> in good works; unto God shall you
> return, all together; and He will tell you [the Truth]
> (about what you have been disputing). (5:48)

There is a clear assumption in this verse that certain basic moral requirements are demanded of all human beings, regardless of differences in religious beliefs. Interestingly enough, the ideal human being is conceived as combining moral virtue with complete religious surrender:

> Nay, but whosoever submits his will to God,
> [while] being a good-doer, his wage is with his Lord,
> and no fear shall be on them, neither shall they sorrow. (2:112)

Undoubtedly we have here a clear basis for a distinction between religion and morality in the Qur'an, where moral virtues are further strengthened by the religious act of submission to sacred authority. It is in the realm of universal moral truth that human beings are treated equally and held equally responsible for responding to universal guidance. Furthermore, this fundamental moral equality of all human beings at the level of universal guidance makes it plausible to maintain that the Qur'an does manifest something akin to the Western notion of natural law:

> By the soul, and That which shaped it
> and inspired it to [know the difference between] lewdness and godfearing.

Fazlur Rahman's translation, although innovative, is close to the statement of the Qur'an:

Freedom of Conscience and Religion in the Qu'ran

> [I swear] by man's personality and that
> whereby it has been formed, God has engraved
> into it its evil and its good [whereby it can
> guard itself against moral peril]. He who
> makes his personality pure, shall be
> successful, while he who corrupts it shall
> be in the loss. (91:7–10)[12]

Fundamentals of Righteous Action

The source of universal guidance is the inherent capacity in man to believe in God. It is something that was connected with the very creation of man as a creature possessing personal responsibility, and presupposes choice and free volition on his part. The Qur'an calls it *fitra*[13] in the following statement:

> So set thy face to the religion,
> a man of pure faith—God's original (*fitra*), [creation]
> upon which He (patterned) mankind. (30:29)

If the above verse is read in conjunction with the statement about the "engraved soul," a clear understanding of *fitra* emerges; namely, that it is that inherent capacity or disposition with which man was created and by virtue of which he is able to grasp universal moral truths. Since the constitutive elements of the term *fitra* come close in signification to what Thomas Aquinas would call *synderesis*, it is important to discuss at some length the views of some exegetes concerning the term.[14]

The Ash'arite theologian-exegete al-Razi, in line with the Ash'arite proclivity toward theistic subjectivism, interprets *fitra* as that which compels a person to affirm the unity of God (*al-tawhid*). Such an interpretation rules out the notion that man is in possession of a choice and free volition in the matter of faith, since it does not allow for a personal responsibility to develop *taqwa*, that sharp moral consciousness spoken of earlier.[15] On the other hand, al-Zamakhshari, consistent with the Mu'tazilite theory of rationalist objectivism, interprets *fitra* as *khilqa*, natural disposition, in the sense that God has created in man a capacity to affirm his unity and accept Islam. This interpretation, contends al-Zamakhshari, is valid on the grounds that there is a concurrence between *fitra* and reasoning, and a harmony between *fitra* and sound opinion (*al-nazar al-sahih*). In other words, *fitra* is as objective and universal as reasoning, and, as such, *fitra* is the capacity to exercise rational choice in the matter of faith. This view of *fitra* is corroborated by the Qur'anic notion that guidance by means of revelation is preceded by a universal guidance available to humanity as originally created by God. Thus, 30:29 commands a person to set his face to the religion (i.e., to respond affirmatively to the call to faith) as one who possesses "upright nature," or the nature (*fitra*) shaped by God, in which he created humankind. This leaves no doubt that *fitra* is an innate disposition and inherent capacity which enables a person to accept or reject faith.

It is in this light that the verse "No compulsion is there in religion" (2:256) should be understood. If the function of religious guidance through revelation is to provide precepts and examples to all men and women in worshiping God and in dealing justly with their fellows (moral virtues), then it presumes an "inward stance" according to which an individual accepts personal responsibility for upholding its directives. This inward stance is the source of the unbated sense of personal responsibility, the natural faith (*al-iman al-fitri*),[16] which lies at the heart of any religious and moral commitment. The Qur'an refers to this inward stance as an essential prerequisite from which a concrete religious submission can be derived:

> The Bedouins say: "We believe."
> Say: "You do not believe; rather
> say "We surrender" (*aslamna*); for belief (*iman*)
> has not yet entered your hearts. (49:14)

This passage clearly differentiates between *islam* ("submission") and *iman* ("faith"), that is, between a submission to sacred authority that might be coerced or compelled by human beings (and consequently become mere utterance of the formula of faith without any commitment to uphold God's commands), and the faith born of voluntary consent, free of human coercive interference, developing from a keen spiritual and moral awareness and motivation. The faith that has "entered the heart" is the result of a choice innately available to all human beings, which is then strengthened and assisted by revelation. In this sense, faith is something freely negotiated directly between God and a person and cannot be compelled, as the Qur'an declares:

> And if thy Lord had willed, whoever
> is in the earth would have believed,
> all of them, all together. Wouldst thou [O Muhammad]
> then constrain the people, until
>   they are believers?
> *It is not for any soul to believe*
> *save by the leave of God;* and He lays
> abomination upon those who have
>   no understanding. (10:99–100)

Indeed, even the Prophet, the bearer of revealed guidance, should not compel the people to believe. According to the above passage it is God who grants or withholds the gift of faith, who either makes the heart receptive to warnings or hardens it upon unsatisfactory actions or attitudes on the part of an individual. Religious devotion, then, is something no one can supply for anybody else. At one point, when the Prophet becomes frustrated with the refusal of the Meccan people to respond to the faith, the Qur'an consoles him with a reminder:

> We have not sent the Koran upon thee
> for thee to be (miserable), but only
> as a reminder to
> him who fears [the final judgement]. (20:2)

Or, in another place:

> Yet perchance, if they believe not
> in this tiding, thou wilt consume
> thyself, following after them, of
> grief [that they do not believe]. (18:6)

This is an extremely important observation about the teaching of the Qur'an. It is precisely this understanding of religion that Little has highlighted in respect to Roger Williams. According to Williams, a person has a right to erroneous religious belief, and that person may not be punished or coerced, nor deprived of civil rights and liberties, on account of religious conviction. Such a conclusion appears to be confirmed by the Qur'anic utterance: "No compulsion is there in religion" (2:256).

It is important to see the way that Muslim exegetes have interpreted the "No compulsion" verse. It is, in my opinion, perhaps the most profound statement of the Qur'an on basic individual freedom in matters of religion. Curiously, the exegetes have interpreted the verse as implying that only the People of the Book—i.e., Jews, Christians, and Zoroastrians—should be left to their own religion, so long as they pay the *jizya* (poll tax), while the Arabs who did not possess a revealed religion must be forced to accept Islam at the point of a sword. Al-Tabari, in his traditional exegesis, cites several reports on the authority of the early associates of the Prophet, which authorize tolerating only the People of the Book. But he does not agree that the "No compulsion" verse was abrogated by the verses that ordained *jihad* (the holy war undertaken to subdue the unbelievers to the rule of Islamic polity, 2:216ff). Al-Tabari argues that while it was the practice (*sunna*) of the Prophet not to force the People of the Book to accept Islam, he did condone compelling the idol worshipers among the Arabs and the apostates (*al-murtaddun*) to accept the faith.

In support of his contention he relates a story of a Muslim belonging to the tribe of Salim b. ʿAwf of Medina, whose two sons had embraced Christianity before Islam was preached. When the sons came to visit their father in Medina, he was grieved for them and asked them to convert to Islam. They refused to do so. The father brought them before the Prophet and asked him to intervene in the controversy. It was on this occasion, according to al-Tabari, that the "No compulsion" verse was revealed, and the father, apparently on the advice of the Prophet, left his two sons alone. The Ashʿarite exegete al-Razi agrees with al-Tabari's conclusion that tolerance in the matter of religion was to be afforded only to the People of the Book, with the implication that others were to be coerced into converting to Islam.[17]

Al-Zamakhshari, the Muʿtazilite exegete, on the other hand, maintains that God does not permit faith through compulsion and coercion, as the Ashʿarites believe. Rather, God allows faith through strengthening a person with *fitra* and free choice (*al-ikhtiyar*). Al-Zamakhshari goes on to quote 10:99 in support of his assertion:

> And if thy Lord had willed, whoever
> is in the earth would have believed,
> all of them, all together. Wouldst thou [O Muhammad]
> then constrain the people until
> they are believers?

Thus, al-Zamakhshari says, if God had willed, he would have compelled them to believe; however, he did not do this and instead allowed people to have free choice in the matter of faith.[18] Like al-Tabari, al-Zamakhshari cites all other opinions, including the story of the Muslim from the tribe of Salim b. ʿAwf.

However, the implications of the "No compulsion" verse for al-Zamakhshari are in conformity with his overall rationalist view. Not only are the People of the Book not to be coerced in converting to Islam; *all* human beings must have the basic right to exercise free volition in this matter. Accordingly, the verse does not set a limit so that "No compulsion in religion" is to be applied exclusively to the People of the Book. Moreover, the story cited in support of the interpretation of al-Tabari and others does not end with a declaration from the Prophet that only the People of the Book were to be spared in the matter of accepting Islam by coercion. Indeed, the story appears to confirm our conclusions about the role of *fitra* and its implications for religious belief.

Thus *fitra* becomes the source of that natural guidance created by God which, if not impaired by unsatisfactory actions or attitudes, will lead to the acceptance and strengthening of faith through revealed guidance. More importantly *fitra* establishes human responsibility in heeding the directives of the universal guidance, which in turn requires an act of free volition in order to guard the *fitra* in an unimpaired state. That the latter is part of human responsibility is implicit in the Qur'anic teaching about the Day of Judgment when God will not punish anyone for an act for which he or she is not responsible.

The innate disposition, then, has always to be kept in a sound state if it is to be confirmed and enhanced by revealed guidance; failure to guard it results in the hardening of the heart, which the Qur'an calls the "sick heart":

> When the hypocrites, and those in whose
> heart was sickness, said, "Their religion
> has deluded them;" but whosoever
> puts his trust in God, surely God is
> All-mighty, All-wise. (8:49)

The term "heart" (*qalb,* plural *qulub*) is frequently used in the Qur'an in the sense of the seat of consciousness, thoughts, volition, and feeling. As such, "heart" seems to be the receptacle of the *fitra,* that inherent capacity which is affected by the choice made in the matter of faith. When a person rejects guidance and strays away from the true path, then the heart becomes veiled and is deprived of understanding:

> And who does greater evil than he
> who, being reminded of signs
> of his Lord, turns away from them and
> forgets what his hands have forwarded?
> Surely We have laid veils on their hearts
> lest they understand it, and in their ears heaviness;
> and though thou callest them to the
> guidance, yet they will not be guided ever. (18:57)

When the heart becomes veiled, it loses the capacity to confront the deep questions of final authority and destiny, and it loses the capacity to fulfill its nature. The heart thus appears to be the faculty for distinguishing truth from falsehood, good from evil, beneficial from harmful. It discovers the benefit of revealed guidance, which reminds it that God commands that good be done and evil be avoided, and sets out to obey the religious and moral ordinances:

> Surely in that [the revelation] there is a reminder to him
> who has a heart, or will give ear with a present mind. (50:37)

The act of believing and following the path makes the heart attain the state of bliss at the remembrance of the source of this guidance—that is, God:

> Those who believe, their hearts being at rest
> in God's remembrance—in God's remembrance
> are at rest the hearts of those who believe
> and do righteous deeds; their is blessedness and a fair resort. (13:28)

The heart in the Qur'an thus signifies the instrument of religious and moral perception which has the ability to make ultimate judgments in keeping with the *fitra,* that nature with which humankind is created. So understood, the heart is *al-damir,* a notion very close to the concept of conscience. Having discerned universal religious and moral truths according to the *fitra,* it is able to guide a person faced with religious and moral dilemmas. When the heart responds to revealed guidance by embracing faith, it becomes the pure or sound heart which has been softened and made healthy by God's inspiration. On the other hand, when it fails to respond to revelation, it becomes a sick heart that is hardened to God's direction.

> . . . He shows you
> His signs, that haply you may have understanding.
> Then your hearts became hardened thereafter
> and are like stones, or even yet harder;
> for there are stones from which rivers come gushing. . . . (2:73–74)

In some important ways the above description of the notion and background of the concept "heart" in the Qur'an comes close to Little's analysis of conscience in Western thought. Like the relationship between *synderesis* and conscience, the heart, with its seat in the *fitra,* draws upon the cognitive and normative capacities available to it through universal guidance and undertakes to resolve those practical and spiritual dilemmas that confront a person. If the Western idea of conscience involves the resolution of practical conflicts through the rendering of a judgment of approval or disapproval concerning the pertinent courses of action, and through the determining of the degree of individual responsibility for taking the right or wrong course,[19] the heart appears to play an analogous role in Qur'anic thought. By means of that universal guidance which is embedded in the innate disposition (*fitra*), an individual determines the sort of response he or she will make to fundamental spiritual and moral requirements, as well as to the consequences of taking one action or another. The person who possesses heart, according to the Qur'an, also possesses understanding. That person has the cognitive power of grasping and reflecting on certain basic objective and universal religious and moral truths. In addition, such a person is guided by engraved normative nature (91:8) and possesses the affective disposition to feel certain special emotions in respect to choices made and actions taken. The Qur'an frequently speaks of how an individual will call to mind what he has been striving for (79:35), and how the ultimate outcome of the individual's choices are affected by preoccupation with short-term, selfish, narrow, and material concerns at the expense of the loftier requirements of a life of devotion and righteousness (69:19–29). This calling to mind is often pricked by certain painful emotional experiences, parallel to the Western pangs of conscience. Finally, an individual has the opportunity, by means of a conative disposition, to seek what the heart believes to be good and to shun what it believes to be evil; to begin, at least, to achieve the goal of life—final prosperity.[20]

Implications of Universal and Revelational Guidance in the Qur'an

The foregoing discussion of the two forms of guidance maintained in the Qur'an provides us with the basis for a Qur'anic understanding of human destiny, and of God's way of directing human beings to it. It also makes abundantly clear that the Qur'an, by means of its notion of a universal guidance engraved upon human nature, teaches that individuals are in possession of dispositions that make room for voluntary consent in respect to matters of religious belief, such as the doctrine of God and the Day of Judgment as revealed by the Prophet.

That which undergirds the opportunity for human volition is a set of Qur'anic assumptions regarding the existence of objective, universal spiritual and moral truths, and the cognitive, rational, volitional, and affective capacity of human beings to act upon those truths. In the last analysis human beings are confronted with an ultimate choice: "to purify [the soul] and become prosperous, [or] to corrupt it and fail." For his part God, according to the Qur'an, has promised that he will abundantly bestow on all his creatures a quality called guidance, to nurture them until they attain the desirable goal.

Muhammad 'Abduh, one of the most prominent Sunni thinkers of modern times, describes four types of this guidance which God bestows by his grace (lutf) in order to help human beings attain what is ultimately desirable.

1. Guidance which comes though natural mental forces and an innate pro-

pensity or natural disposition. This type of guidance is available to an infant from the time of its birth, as is evident in its inclination to avoid pain and to seek survival without being taught to do so. According to 'Abduh, the infant "knows" these things by means of *fitra*.

2. Guidance which is provided through sensory perception and which actually functions as a development of the first form of guidance. Like the first form it is available to animals as well as human beings. In fact, notes 'Abduh, in animals this guidance is even more complete than in humans. Indeed, sensory capacities and innate impulses in animals are perfected within a short period after they are born, whereas in humans they are perfected gradually.

3. Guidance which is provided through the rational faculty. God, says 'Abduh, created human beings that they might live in society; however, he did not make innate propensities or mental forces sufficient for this purpose, as he did in the case of lower animals, who can manage their affairs by means of the first two forms of guidance. Human beings are in need of more than one type of innate impulse. Consequently God has bestowed on them a form of guidance which is related to the rational faculty and which is superior to the foregoing forms. Human reason is capable of correcting error of perception and of explaining its causes.

4. Guidance which comes through religion—that is, through the message proclaimed through the prophetic medium. The rational faculty is capable of committing errors just as sense organs are. These errors could lead one to apply reason and the knowledge of the senses mistakenly in striving for the goal of life, namely prosperity for oneself and others. In the pursuit of one's lesser appetites a person's guidance could lead him astray and ultimately cause his destruction. It is at such a time, maintains 'Abduh, that religion comes to the aid of people, showing them where they have gone wrong and demonstrating the limits of reason and the futility of pursuing only the appetites. Religion is the light that brings a person out of the darkness caused by his own fallacious judgment:

> God is the Protector of the believers;
> He brings them forth from (darkness [*zulumat*]) into the light.
> And the unbelievers—their protectors are
> (false deities), that bring them forth from the light into the (darkness). (2:257)

Religion also makes one aware of the hereafter, the second life, wherein lies one's permanent abode. It is for this reason, says 'Abduh, that God has bestowed religious guidance in addition to the first three forms of guidance.

Thus, 'Abduh concludes, the meaning of guidance in the Qur'anic passages is directing (*al-dalala*), which is analogous to aiding people at the crossroads of success and failure. It provides a full explanation of the consequences of choosing one path or the other. This guidance, which we have called universal and prior guidance, is given to all human beings equally; whereas additional guidance is given particularly to those who have voluntarily chosen to tread the path of success in order to help them in their strivings and to facilitate their journey on the path of prosperity. This latter guidance is not bestowed on all human beings alike, in the way that guidance through the senses, rational faculty, and innate disposition is given. It is precisely for this reason that a person should ask for this type of guidance, as the Qur'an prescribes in 1:5. Since human beings encounter errors and are misled in their perceptions, they are in need of a special aid which God can confer through prayer: "Guide us in the straight path" (1:5), meaning: "Help us by divine aid so that we remain protected from being misguided and committing errors."[21]

It is worth noting that Muhammad 'Abduh's view of guidance, systematically extracted from the Qur'anic passages and their presuppositions, assumes certain objective, universal values to be imprinted upon the human psyche and the ability of human beings to acquire the necessary knowledge to assume personal responsibility and the consequences thereof. Such assumptions hardly leave room for compulsion in the matter of religion.

However, just as there exists a tension between rationalist objectivism and theistic subjectivism in the matter of the nature of the knowledge of values, there also exists a tension in the question of tolerance of what the Qur'an calls a sick (erroneous) heart, one that has not responded to the "only straight path to God" (16:9)—that is, *islam* "submission." According to the Qur'an, only that path which acknowledges that God is of importance in leading human beings to prosperity is the straight path. All other paths are deviant, and detrimental to the unity of mankind (6:160ff).

The Qur'an acknowledges the diversity of the paths adopted by different people despite the unity of their origins; on the other hand, it declares the superiority of "the true religion with God [which] is Islam" (3:19). In other words, the unity of the path is at the level of universal guidance, that which is imprinted upon human beings by God and by virtue of which they are all one nation. At the same time, diversity exists at the level of the particular guidance proclaimed by the prophets. Accordingly, humankind comes to be divided into different religious communities as its members adhere to one or another revelation. That this diversity is a divinely approved mystery becomes obvious when the Qur'an states:

> The people were one nation; then God sent forth
> the Prophets, good tidings to bear
> and warning, and He sent down with them
> the Book with the truth, that He might
> decide between the people touching their differences;
> and only those who had been given it
> were at variance upon it, after the
> clear signs had come to them [through the Prophets], being insolent
> one to another; then God guided those
> who believed to the truth, touching which
> they were at variance, by His leave;
> and God guides whomsoever He will
> to a straight path. (2:213)

The differences are the result of the people's being "insolent one to another." Ultimately God alone can guide them out of their different beliefs to the truth which is the straight path. Still, the differences, although deplored as originating from human insolence, are tolerated by God, as evidenced in another statement of the Qur'an:

> Had thy Lord willed, He would have mankind
> one nation; but they continue in their differences
> excepting those on whom thy Lord has mercy. (11:118)

In another place even the Prophet is advised to show tolerance toward those who did not accept his message and opposed him:

> And if thy Lord had willed, whoever
> is in the earth would have believed,
> all of them, all together. Wouldst thou [O Muhammad]
> then constrain the people, until
> they are believers? (10:99)

The above verses show that submission to the will of God (*islam*) must come through voluntary consent, which is prompted by the universal guidance that is engraved upon the human heart. Thus, Little's suggestion that "compulsion and external interference [in the matter of genuine devotion to the will of God] would appear to be the antithesis of Islamic faith" is evidently correct. That which leads a person to wander blindly in his insolence is ignorance, as the following passage suggests:

> They have sworn by God the most earnest oaths
> if a sign comes to them they will believe in it.

Freedom of Conscience and Religion in the Qu'ran

> Say: "Signs are only with God." What will make you
> realize that when it comes, they will not believe?
> We shall turn about their hearts and their eyes,
> even as they believed not in it the first time;
> and We shall leave them in their insolence
>   wandering blindly.
> Though We had sent down the angels to them,
> and the dead had spoken with them,
> had We mustered against them every thing, face to face, yet
> they would not have been the ones to believe,
> unless God willed; but most of them are ignorant. (6:109–11)

The necessary underpinning of the above passage is the absolute claim of the Qur'an that guidance is the function of God and that it is he alone who can "turn about their hearts" after their initial rejection of divine guidance. Moreover, their original insolence causes God to deprive human beings of seeing the truth. So in the final analysis the burden of being misguided lies on human shoulders, for despite their knowledge of the requirement to be "forward in good works" (5:48), human beings have chosen to turn their backs upon the guidance received from God (9:38).

Thus, the Qur'an teaches the necessity, on the part of those who have found the right way, to abstain from abusing those who have not done so, and to abstain from compelling them to change their religion. Above all, there is the assurance that the final judgment in the matter of faith rests with God alone and no one else, not even the Prophet:

> Had God willed, they were not
> idolators; and We have not appointed
> thee a watcher over them, neither art
> thou their guardian.
> Abuse not those to whom they pray,
> apart from God, or, they will abuse
> God in revenge without knowledge.
> So We have decked out fair to every
> nation their deeds; then to their Lord
> they shall return, and He will tell
> them what they have been doing. (6:107–108)

The Qur'an emphatically denies any human being the right to take it upon himself to decide for others what Little has accurately described as the "spiritual destiny" of humankind. That is exclusively the domain of the "Master of the Day of Doom" (1:4).

The above discussion of the Qur'anic notion of religious pluralism, even when the right path is conceived as the only basis which God has decreed for uniting humankind, rules out the intolerant claims that religious communities frequently make. By recognizing the capacity for universal righteousness that can be found among the adherents of other religious traditions, the Qur'an sets forth a fundamental principle of religious liberty.

The difference between a moral and a religious obligation is important to bear in mind in this regard, especially in relation to the two forms of guidance, the universal and the particular. On the basis of universal guidance it is appropriate to demand uniformity because an objective and universally binding moral standard is assumed to exist that guarantees true human well-being. Toward the end of enforcing that basic moral standard, resort to compulsion is legitimate. On the basis of particular guidance it is crucial to allow human beings to exercise their volition because the matter of belief, as repeatedly affirmed by the Qur'an, is strictly between individuals and God. So construed, the main function of particular guidance is to remind and warn people, through the proclamation of the divine message, that it is only submission to God's will that will lead them to the real prosperity:

> We know very well what they [unbelievers] say;
> thou art not a (compeller) over them.
> Therefore remind by the Koran him
> who fears My threat. (50:45)

This analysis of guidance reinforces Little's conclusion that the Qur'anic material provides a substantial basis for religious liberty. Not only does the Qur'an maintain the idea of universal and objective moral values; it also upholds the notion of erroneous conscience (the sick heart) that underlies the Western notion of religious liberty.

Apostasy: Religious Liberty and the Social Order in Early Islam

However, over against this liberal spirit there are statements in the Qur'an demanding the use of force in achieving one of the central ideals of Islamic revelation, the creation of a just social order.

In his brilliant work on the Qur'an, Fazlur Rahman has shown that the aim of Islamic ideology, as it emerges from the Qur'an, is to create a just society, to "command good and forbid evil" (3:104,110; 9:71). In Little's terms, this would constitute a moral obligation "taken to be binding upon and available to all," and one to which "all people may be held accountable." Further, Rahman considers the implementation of Islamic theology as representing the social dimensions of *taqwa,* that is, keen moral perception and motivation. Rahman concludes that "with all its concern for a liberal pluralism for institutions and basic individual freedom, the Qur'an, under certain conditions, admits that the state, when representing society, is paramount."[22] Rebellion is punishable by the severest penalties:

> The punishment of those who take up
> arms against God and His messenger
> and devote themselves to [corruption],
> creating discord on the earth, is that
> they should be killed or hung on the
> cross or their hands and feet should be
> severed from the opposite sides or they
> should be exiled—such should be their
> disgrace in this life, and in the hereafter
> there is greater chastisement for them,
> except those who repent before you lay
> your hands upon them. (5:33–34)
> [Rahman's translation]

Accordingly, Rahman believes that the state is assigned to control "discord on earth," a phrase which indicates a general state of lawlessness created by taking up arms against God and his messenger, that is, the established Islamic order. The eradication of corruption on earth, which the Qur'an repeatedly demands, when taken in the light of the Qur'anic principle of commanding good and forbidding evil, thus represents a basic moral requirement to protect the well-being of a community. However, this need not contradict the liberty afforded to individual conscience in matters of faith. This idea—that certain moral requirements form a kind of boundary which is the necessary condition of conscience—was the basis for Roger Williams's justification of the enforcement of civil and moral law by the state, as Little has emphasized.

Nevertheless, such an essential distinction is not only absent in Rahman's exegesis of the Qur'an, it is also lacking in the classical texts on Islamic religious law (the *Shari'a*). Although the essential division of Islamic jurisprudence into *ibadat* (God-person relationship) and *mu'amalat* (person-person relationship) does point to a sort of recognition of religious and interpersonal moral obligations, due to the complexity of the Qur'anic materials the distinction has not been conceptually worked out.[23] The tendency is to collapse religious and moral matters, and thus to treat moral and religious transgressions as equally liable under civil law. This can be illustrated in terms of the treatment of apostates in Islamic religious law. The question of apostasy is particularly important for understanding the discrepancy between the Qur'anic emphasis on religious liberty, as discussed throughout the second part of this chapter, and the intolerant, sometimes even harsh, attitude of Muslim jurists concerning the treatment of apostates. In searching through the penal law of Islam it becomes evident that with the exception of apostasy, no legal penalties are provided for offences against religion as such; they will be dealt with in the hereafter. This exception in regard to apostasy stems from the inability of classical jurists to distinguish the admittedly complex relationship between a moral and a religious action. We must ask why, in view of the Qur'anic evidence, this is so; and we shall see that it is connected with the tension, already identified, between the Qur'an's emphasis on religious liberty and its simultaneous demand for a just social order.

In general Muslim jurists regard the performance of certain acts which have been forbidden in the Qur'an as crimes against religion in the particular sense of violating the "right" or "claim" of God (*haqq allah*). These acts constitute *hudud* offenses for which, according to the jurists, the penalties are established in the Qur'an. Jurists differ as to the number of the *hudud* offenses. Some consider the following seven as *hudud* crimes to be punished by mandatory penalties: unlawful intercourse; false accusation of unlawful intercourse; theft; highway robbery; wine drinking; apostasy, and rebellion. Some jurists omit rebellion, while others restrict the list to the first four crimes, for which the Qur'an prescribes specific penalties.[24] These latter classify wine drinking and apostasy as *ta'zir* offenses, meaning crimes for which there are no specified penalties in the Qur'an and for which it is left to the ruler or judge to determine *ta'zir* (chastisement) in accordance with the public interest, taking into account changing conditions and times.[25] In the case of apostasy, it must be pointed out, there is general agreement among the jurists that, while the perception that it is a crime stems from the Qur'an, the assignment of the death penalty stems from the prophetic *hadith* report which says: "Whoever changes his religion, kill him," and is sanctioned by the consensus (*ijma'*) of the early associates of the Prophet.[26] Hence, it is accurate to maintain that although this punishment is not properly speaking *hadd* (i.e., 'fixed' because of the absence of any specific text in the Qur'an sanctioning the death penalty for apostasy), it is regarded as such by some jurists because apostasy involves the claim of God. This being the case, the punishment of apostates becomes necessary for the protection of a fundamental public interest: the creation and maintenance of a just social order.[27]

But how does apostasy, as a religious act, come to be so tied to the question of public order? The problem of defining an act of apostasy in Islam goes back to the early days of the caliphate, specifically to the wars of *ridda* ("apostasy," more accurately "secession"). Apostasy, as it came to be defined in the Islamic legal writings of the Classical Period (ninth and tenth centuries), signified rejection of Islam by word, deed, or omission. Rejection of Islam by word meant to deny God's existence and other doctrines of Islamic faith, including any part of the Qur'an or its main tenets such as prayer and almsgiving (*zakat*); rejection of Islam by deed meant acting contrary to its teachings; rejection by omission meant refraining from performance of an act required by the Qur'an.

There is an underlying concern in these definitions of apostasy. That is, as an attitude demonstrated either verbally or by a public act, apostasy infringes on private or community interests in the public order. Accordingly, the jurists have held that it is the duty of public authorities, such as the imam or caliph, to lay down punishments for it. The demand for a society incorporating the spirit of the Qur'an thus gives rise to an important tension in connection with the idea of religious liberty.

The two emphases pull in conflicting directions. On the one hand, properly understood, religious belief in the Qur'an is beyond the reach of human coercion. Indeed, to punish or constrain people because of their religious beliefs is, it would seem, simply to distract them from the voluntary basis of true religious belief and practice by introducing an external or alien motive for living a religious life. To believe, or to say one does, out of fear of punishment is, according to the Qur'an, not authentic belief at all, but hypocrisy—something devoutly to be resisted.

On the other hand, the Qur'an appears to say that part of establishing a desirable political community, one that conforms with the wishes of God, is to constrain, by force if necessary, those who, as the Qur'an puts it, "take up arms" or "exhibit enmity" against God. Not only did the Prophet deliver the divine message to the people; he also founded a state intended to uphold the sociopolitical implications of his message. The consequence of this, as it has traditionally been understood, is that certain forms of religious expression and practice—particularly apostasy—or public denunciation or rejection of the fundamental tenets of Islamic faith—are regarded as a (moral) threat to the public security of the community. Accordingly, such hostile religious acts must be treated with the same severity as other, more clearly moral threats to the security of the community, such as rebellion, theft, highway robbery, and the like. The tension, then, is this: Religious belief at the same time both may and may not be subjected to civil liabilities.

While it is true that this tension lies in the message of the Qur'an, and that it is nowhere more sharply focused than on the subject of apostasy, we can go at least some distance toward clearing up a number of the confusions that appear to have attached themselves to the subject of apostasy.

The earliest reference to an act of apostasy from Islam occurs in connection with the breach of agreement between the Islamic authorities in Medina and a number of Arab tribes, following the death of the Prophet. I wish to demonstrate, in the light of the evidence gathered from Islamic historical and religious sources, that the campaign undertaken by Abu Bakr in his capacity as the head of the Medina government against these seceding tribes does not involve a case of apostasy at all. Therefore, its citation as a valid precedent for the definition and punishment of apostasy has no justification. Let us turn to the evidence concerning these so-called "wars of apostasy" (ridda).

The sources show that following the Prophet's death in A.D. 632 the young Muslim community went through the most difficult and dangerous of times. Abu Bakr, who succeeded Muhammad as the head of the community, was threatened with a split among the leading members of the community, on the one hand, and the rise of a number of Arab tribes against the centralization of political authority in Medina, on the other. Under these circumstances Abu Bakr indignantly rejected the demand of the Arab tribes that they be released from paying the zakat tax, and ordered his army to march against them. After much bloodshed the revolts were suppressed, and the tribes were brought again under the dominion of Medina. This early episode in Abu Bakr's reign provided the fundamental precedent for the law of apostasy in Islam.

Consideration of the letters and recommendations sent to the dissenting tribes makes it clear that Abu Bakr, in his attempt to bring the tribes under the power of Islamic polity, strongly emphasized the agreement the tribes had made with a prophet appointed by God.[28] Of course, Muhammad was not merely the head of a state; he was a prophet appointed by God. The strictly religious aspect of his position was a prime concern of the Qur'an. It was also a prime concern for the rulers of Medina, whose authority could only be religiously legitimized through their position as successors to the Prophet—the representative of divine authority on earth, appointed to accomplish the purpose for which the Qur'an was revealed in the first place. Thus, while Abu Bakr reminded the tribesmen that Muhammad was a mortal being, he did not forget to emphasize that God, whom Muhammad represented, was "the Living and the Everlasting God" (2:255). They should consider their agreement as being with God and honor it as long as there remained the authority (i.e., the Medina government) that carried on the function of Muhammad as the messenger of God.[29]

Freedom of Conscience and Religion in the Qu'ran

In all these communications to the tribes asking them to hold to their agreement with the Islamic polity, Abu Bakr did not produce any Qur'anic verses that would certify the severe measures he could take against them on the basis of sanctions provided by God—verses such as Muslim jurists in the subsequent periods used to justify the death penalty for apostastes. The absence of such Qur'anic documentation to justify his severe measures shows that there was nothing in the Qur'an that could sanction his political solution to the growing dissent among the tribesmen. Moreover, for Abu Bakr the crucial matter was the recognition of Medina's authority as the continuation of the prophetic authority that had been challenged by the tribes who had refused to pay the *zakat* tax.

Indeed, it should be said that there are no Qur'anic passages that specifically sanction the execution of apostates. In his *War and Peace in the Law of Islam*, Majid Khadduri cites 4:88–89, which deals with hypocrites, and all the major commentators state that the passage apparently refers to those Arabs who used to come to Medina and declare themselves to be Muslims and on their return to Mecca would revert to their pagan beliefs and engage in hostile acts against the Muslim community. Consequently, the Qur'an says:

> If they (turn back [to enmity] then)
> take them, and slay them wherever you find them,
> (and choose no protector nor helper from among them). (4:89)

From Abu Bakr's communications it is evident that neither the above passage nor any other citation from the Qur'an was used to justify his action. It was important for him to remind the tribes about their commitment to God, the only immortal being, and to say that under no circumstances would the successor of Muhammad regard the agreement between the tribes and Muhammad as canceled. Consequently, the tribes would be forced to honor their commitment and would be brought under the dominion of Medina (i.e., to pay *zakat*), even if it led to the use of force.

This brings us to the consideration of the question of the death penalty for apostasy. As pointed out above, Abu Bakr did not produce—and in fact was not in need of producing—a Qur'anic justification for his solution to the political turmoil created by the Prophet's death. Consequently, the verses cited in justification for Abu Bakr's solution are not taken from those passages in which God reserves his right to be the sole judge in dealing with unbelief among the people. The justification rather lies in those verses which establish the duties of Muslims (religious and moral) in connection with the imperative to establish a just public order.

It must be emphasized that for Abu Bakr the punishment inflicted upon the

Arab tribes apparently involved a case of rebellion against the Islamic public order, and not, as it subsequently came to be interpreted by Muslim legal scholars, a case of apostasy, of violating the right of God (*haqq allah*). In the latter case only God would have the right to inflict punishment. It was probably for this reason that Abu Bakr did not resort to the apostasy verses in justifying his policy. On the other hand, the Qur'an had left clear instructions regarding the treatment of rebellion which is tantamount to taking up arms against God and his messenger. The passage reads:

> The punishment of those who take up arms
> against God and His Messenger and devote
> themselves to [corruption], creating
> discord on earth, is that they should
> be killed or hung on the cross or their
> hands and feet should be severed from the
> opposite sides or they should be exiled. (5:33)

Taking up arms against God seems to pull in conflicting directions. On the one hand, the phrase clearly suggests a crime of a religious nature, committed directly against God. No human agency has any authority to punish or constrain those who take up arms against God in that sense. On the other hand, the passage suggests that enmity to God is primarily a political crime—"creating discord on earth." Moreover, it is a political crime committed against the head of the Islamic public order. This is corroborated by the fact that the passage also speaks about taking up arms against the Prophet, who is not only the messenger of God but also the political head of Medina. Taking up arms against God and his messenger has been interpreted by all the major exegetes of the Qur'an as violation of public security by engaging in acts that cause fear in the hearts of people, such as highway robbery. Tabari, for instance, mentions several interpretations of the phrase, one of which explicitly states that to take up arms against God and his messenger implies "violation of the terms of contract, highway robbery, and spread of corruption."[30] It is evident that whereas violation of the terms of contract and highway robbery could be categorized as moral offences threatening the welfare of the people, spread of corruption, which might be attributed to unbelievers in the Qur'an, could mean a religious violation causing deviation from Islamic tenets and hence resulting in moral deterioration. This connection helps to explain the "running together" of religious and public order concerns. Nevertheless, the tension between these two concerns remains, and needs to be exposed more fully.

My contention is that this tension has not been explored fully enough by traditional jurisprudence. From the evidence presented, it appears that the use of Abu Bakr's campaign against the Arab tribes as a precedent in support of the sanction against apostasy is unwarranted. Moreover, I believe that it was the inclusion of this precedent as evidence which led to apostasy being the only religious crime for which capital punishment was assigned in the penal law. The Muslim jurists, like the early Muslim leaders, did not sufficiently appreciate the tension between the religious and the moral, or spiritual and temporal, in the Qur'an; this led them too readily to classify disobedience to certain duties enjoined by the laws of Islamic polity as unbelief, thereby treating this disobedience as a threat to the well-being of the community, and therefore as apostasy.[31] The Arab tribes had more evidently committed a political crime, whereby the welfare of other individuals in the society, or even the stability of the state, was endangered. Accordingly, the episode is highly questionable as a precedent for the law concerning apostasy. Whereas I do concede the existence of a complex relationship between the strictly religious and the moral in the Qur'an, I believe that obscuring this distinction led to an excessively intolerant tone in the Islamic legal system, a tone that has greatly affected Muslim practice in everyday life.

The subsequent rationalization of the death penalty for apostasy in Islamic penal law is in direct conflict with the Qur'anic spirit of religious liberty. On the other hand, if the death penalty is seen in the context of Abu Bakr's attempt to establish his authority as the political head of the politicoreligious community, and of the deep threat to the Islamic public order which he perceived to be involved by the defection of Arab tribes, then there seems to have been sufficient Qur'anic justification to deal severely with those individuals engaging in "spreading corruption on earth." There remains a gray area for religion and morality in terms of the proper location of "corruption" in an Islamic system of justice. Nevertheless, it is not possible, on the basis of our discussion, to define Abu Bakr's campaign as a case involving a religious offence in the strict sense. Evidently through his political action Abu Bakr was seeking an explicit recognition of his position as the legitimate successor of the Prophet, a recognition that would enhance his religious control of the Islamic order. However, there is no hard evidence to show that Abu Bakr in his campaigns against the tribes made any religious claims—at least to justify his severe measures. This latter point further corroborates my contention regarding the doubtful status of the episode as a precedent for the punishment of apostasy in the penal law. (For further discussion see Appendix 1.)

Jihad and the Conduct of a Muslim State

Closely related to the issue of capital punishment for apostasy in Islamic law is the question of *jihad*—the holy war—which can be seen as a logical outcome of the Qur'anic program of eradicating "corruption on the earth" and of "enjoining the good and forbidding the evil." In the light of the implementation of this program, it is plausible to speak of a moral basis for *jihad* that does not interfere with freedom of conscience, just as it is possible to speak of a legitimate use of force by the state in terms of sustaining public order. Indeed, according to the Mulsim exegetes, *jihad* occurred for the first time in Medina when the Muslims were given permission to fight back with the "people who broke their solemn pledges":

> Will you not fight a people who broke their (solemn pledges)
> and purposed to expel the Messenger,
> (and did attack you first?)? (9:13)

Again

> If they withdraw not
> from you, and offer you peace, and restrain
> their hands, take them, and slay them wherever
> you come on them; against them We have given you
> a clear authority. (4:91)

It is not at all difficult here to perceive a strictly moral justification for the permission given to the Muslims to retaliate with force against attacks upon them. However, as Fazlur Rahman has pointed out, one does not always find in Islamic history a consistent justification for *jihad* on the basis of the Qur'an.[32] In fact, as seen above, the Qur'an justifies defensive *jihad* only. It always speaks of the hostile unbelievers who are to be subdued as dangerous or faithless. Undoubtedly there were many instances of *jihad* in Islamic history in which the actual motivation was an interest in territorial expansion.

Muslim exegetes realized the tension between the demand that the Muslim community strive to make "God's cause succeed" (9:41) and the unmistakable claim, "No compulsion is there in religion." If *jihad* is comprehended within the consistent Qur'anic emphasis on human volition in the matter of faith, then sanctioning the use of force against moral and civil offenses cannot be regarded as contradicting the "No compulsion" verse. On the contrary, this emphasis removes any doubt concerning the purpose of *jihad*. In the light of the "No compulsion" verse, the holy war cannot be anything but "commanding the good and forbidding the evil," the enforcing of obligations that, according to Little have to do with basic moral requirements and not the spiritual destiny of an individual. In other words, the Qur'an sanctions *jihad* as a way of establishing an order that will protect the basic welfare of the Muslim community against both internal and external enemies—that is, the tyrants, those who take up arms against God and his messenger (4:33), and the unbelievers, those who break their oaths (9:13) and thereby threaten the temporal security of the Islamic state.

So construed, to advocate the use of force by an Islamic state in the name of *jihad* or *hudud* would require a clear demonstration that basic moral violations have indeed occurred. In other words, Muslim authorities, whether political or juridical, must conscientiously shoulder the burden of proof and show the Muslim community, whom they represent, that any decision to use compulsion in matters impinging on a person's faith is in no way aimed at changing that person's belief, but simply at enforcing basic moral and civic requirements.

Conclusion

Two general points are, in closing, worth stressing. First, in studying Islamic concepts, it is worth while to remember that in the linear progression of time characterized by historical process Islam developed as a religious phenomenon only after it was established as a political reality. As I have emphasized, early political events and exigencies shaped the subsequent interpretation of Islamic ideology, often without regard for fairly obvious Qur'anic teaching.

The early years of Islam were characterized by a constant succession of victories on the part of the Muslim army under the rulership of the caliphs. Such achievements undoubtedly affected the community's understanding of the *jihad* and the use of force, as they also affected its understanding of the Qur'anic provisions for religious freedom. In the face of the expansion of Islamic political power and hegemony, the deep Qur'anic impulse toward religious freedom steadily lost ground—in practice and in theory—to the equally strong concern for defending the faith against active persecution and violent assault. The defensive use of force gradually gave way to more aggressive legal and political policies.

Second, although Little's chapter is written cautiously, as is seemly in a comparative effort such as this, his principal claim seems correct: The notions that underlie existing international human rights formulations in regard to freedom of religion and conscience are indeed relevant to cultures outside the West, including, it cannot be doubted, Islamic culture. There are, without question, significant differences between the West and Islam in these matters.

These are of course the result of a variety of dissimilar cultural and historical experiences. But there are also, as I have tried to show, striking and revealing commonalities. If it is true that basic individual freedom in religion is a logical requirement of the Qur'anic notion of universal guidance, something which is "engraved" upon the human psyche and which presupposes the ability of all human beings to accept or reject faith, then it hardly matters where and when a given individual comes into existence. Such a right is universally guaranteed to him by his Creator. I have, I believe, sufficiently demonstrated that the Western notions of natural law and conscience are present in the spiritual and ethical utterances and presuppositions of the Qur'an, although the exact terms and their systematic expositions do not appear there, because of the nature of the Islamic revelation. Islamic revelation, as I have indicated above, does not treat spiritual and moral as two separate categories derived from two separate sources. Rather, it treats both as springing from the same source, namely God. Hence, it posits a complex relationship between the realms of morality and religion: a relationship which, with careful analysis, I believe it is possible—and important—to distinguish and discuss. The complexity of dealing with the relation of these realms in Qur'anic terms is well demonstrated with reference to the question of apostasy in Islam. Moreover, in discussing the question of divine guidance I have shown, in terms of a variety of classical as well as modern exegeses of the Qur'an, that in the notions of *fitra* (innate disposition) and *qalb* (the heart) we have the constitutive elements of Western notions of *synderesis* and conscience, with important implications for questions of religious liberty.

Further, in my discussion of the theological and ethical implications of the Qur'anic teachings, I have shown that the Qur'an maintains the universality and objectivity of basic spiritual and moral truths, and hence shares the Western understanding that in respect to matters of conscience all human beings are not only equal but equally accountable for any violations. It is, therefore, correct to conclude with confidence that there is much concurrence regarding the underlying commitments of Islam and the West in respect to religious liberty. Both traditions share a common framework within which human beings may think about freedom of conscience and religious liberty.

NOTES

1. James P. Piscatori fails to take into consideration the ethicoreligious implications of the Qur'anic teaching within its sociohistorical context when dealing with freedom of religion. His

treatment of the question of apostasy, for instance, does not take into account the difficulty faced by the founders of major schools of religious law in justifying the death penalty, when in the Qur'an the apostate is threatened with punishment in the next world only. Piscatori, "Human Rights in Islamic Political Culture," *The Moral Imperatives of Human Rights,* ed. Kenneth W. Thompson (Washington: University Press of America, 1980), 145–47.

2. George F. Hourani, "The Ethical Presuppositions of the Qur'an," *The Muslim World* 70 (1980): 1–28.

3. A. J. Arberry, *The Koran Interpreted* (New York: Macmillan, 1955). This is by far one of the most adequately translated versions in English. The title clearly suggests the inclusion of his own understanding of the text when translated. I have used his translation, except in some cases where I have added my explanation in brackets, or revised his translation to conform with the original. Fazlur Rahman, *Major Themes of the Qur'an* (Chicago: Bibliotheca, 1980). The interpretation of the Qur'an in this work demonstrates subjective exegesis at its height.

4. It is also possible to distinguish a philosophical approach to the Qur'anic exegesis—in the work of Ibn Rushd (Averroes), for instance. He exemplifies this approach when he systematically argues that revealed religion is a derivation of absolute religion which contains the absolute truth, that is, the philosophical truth. However, the entire Qur'an is not systematically and uniformly interpreted so as to enable us to trace the historical development of the main ideas that ought to be investigated for the present study.

5. George F. Hourani, *Islamic Rationalism: The Ethics of Abd al-Jabbar* (Oxford: Clarendon, 1971), 3.

6. It is impossible to go into further detail about exegetical materials in this chapter. However, it is worth noting that in the modern exegesis of the Qur'an it was the Mu'tazilite mode that was preferred over the traditional and the Ash'arite ones, especially in connection with the source of knowledge of ethical values. One of the most remarkable exegeses is the one by Muhammad 'Abduh (1849–1905), whose views on the source of natural guidance will be discussed below. His commentary *al-Manar,* which was presented in the form of lectures at the prestigious al-Azhar University in Cairo, and later, compiled and continued by his disciple Rashid Rida, is based on the Mu'tazilite foundation. Hence, it is not surprising to find Hourani, Fazlur Rahman, and many other scholars of the Qur'an stressing the basic rationalist objectivism of the Mu'tazilites by upholding the responsibility of free men before a just God.

7. *Hudan* and *hidaya* (guidance) are identical in meaning except that in the usage of the Qur'an *hudan* usually implies revelational guidance, i.e., regarding the Book and the religious ordinances (*al-Shari'a*). See al-Turayhi, *Majma' al-bahrayn* (Najaf, 1959) 1:472. *Hidaya* is more general in meaning and includes guidance in all matters—social, moral, etc. It is used in the sense of *'ARF* in its second form *'arrafa,* meaning "to apprise." This form is not used in the Qur'an, but was common in the Hijaz, where the Qur'an was revealed. See al-Zabidi, *Taj al-'arus* (Kuwait, 1969), 10:406.

8. I have preferred this translation of *taqwa,* with slight variation, which Fazlur Rahman gives in his *Major Themes,* 56. In fact, he has offered different though similar definitions of *taqwa* in several places. I have a problem with one of them; on p. 29 he equates *taqwa* with the term "conscience." As we shall see below, there is a possibility, on the basis of the Qur'anic usage, of discovering that conscience could become impaired or unsound through its unsatisfactory response to the normative human nature; whereas it is impossible, again on the basis of the Qur'anic usage, to suggest that *taqwa* could become impaired or sick. On p. 57 Rahman speaks about the heart, the "instrument of perception, discernment," as he calls it, which is "dulled," and which loses the "capacity to ask right questions." Considering the way in which the concept

Islam and Religious Liberty

of conscience is explained in the Western ethical literature, it is more probable to relate "heart" in the Qur'an ("the mind," as Rahman translates it in 22:45–46), to the conscience, because of the possibility of describing it as the sick or sound heart. On the other hand, the translation of *taqwa* as "keen [spiritual and] moral perception and motivation" is more accurate considering the verses in which the concept appears in the Qur'an. In that sense *taqwa* can be regarded as an all-encompassing aspect of sound conscience.

9. Even the Ash'ari exegete al-Razi, who maintains complete subordination of human will to the divine will, recognizes two forms of guidance: first, guidance by means of *dalil* (demonstration) and *hujja* (proof or evidence), both activities of the human rational faculty, which he considers limited; and second, guidance through inner purification of the soul and ascetic practices. He does not speak of revelation as a separate form of guidance; rather, as an Ash'ari, he considers revelation (i.e., the will of God) to superimpose all forms of guidance. See his *Tafsir* (Cairo, 1938), 1:9ff.

10. Ibn Manzur, *Lisan al-'arab*, 13/457–58; al-Firuzabadi, *al-Qamus al-muhit*, 1/432, 2/415–16; al-Zabidi, *Taj al-'arus* 8/9–10.

11. Ibn Manzur, *Lisan al-'arab*, 13/458; see also E. W. Lane, *Arabic-English Lexicon*, 1/4, 1972–75.

12. Rahman, *Major Themes*, 24. It is worthwhile to compare Roger Williams's views about the fundamental moral truths that underlie his influential formulations about freedom of conscience in the Western context, as discussed by Little, with the above observation about the Qur'anic teaching. There is a remarkable similarity between his concept of natural law with its objectivity and universality binding moral truths (that it is "imprinted upon the human psyche") and what we have called universal guidance on the basis of explicit and implicit Qur'anic statements concerning man's normative nature "engraved upon his soul."

13. *Fitra* means "creation." The verb *FTR* is used in this sense in the Qur'an in 11:51: "O My people! I do not ask of you a wage for this. My wage falls only upon Him who did originate me (*fatarani*)." It has the meaning of bringing something into existence, newly, for the first time. *Fitra* in the Qur'an and the *hadith* literature signifies the natural constitution with which a child is created in his mother's womb; it also signifies the faculty of knowing God, with which he endowed humankind, and whereby a person acquires an inherent capacity or innate disposition to accept the religion of truth. See Lane, *Lexicon*, 1/6, 2416. The evolution of the meaning of *fitra* from "creation" to "natural law" can be attributed to the theological dispute concerning the fate of children who die before reaching adulthood. The conflict between the tradition about the natural religions with which every child is born and the doctrine of predestination was obvious, and the theologians had to attempt exegetical resolution of the problem. In the end, the explanation that "every child is born with a disposition toward Islam" was favored over other explanations that supported the predestinarian view of belief and unbelief. See A. J. Wensinck, *Muslim Creed* (London: Frank Cass, 1965), 42–44, 214–16.

14. See, e.g., John Donnelly's essay, "Conscience and Religious Morality," *Conscience*, ed. John Donnelly and Leonard Lyons (New York: Alba House, 1973), where he traces the theories of Ockam and Aquinas on the role of conscience in ethical reasoning. Of great relevance to *fitra* is the explanation of *synderesis* as understood by Aquinas in the context of arriving at a practical judgment of reason on the matter of resolving the duties imposed by the Law of God: ". . . *synderesis*, which is the disposition by virtue of which one grasps the most general principles of morality. It is accordingly an infallible and innate disposition that enables us to grasp certain basic moral principles" (164–65).

15. al-Razi, *Tafsir* 25/121ff.

16. I have adopted this phrase from al-Razi, *Tafsir*, 25/120, where he believes this to be sufficient for the proper affirmation of the unity of God as explained in the revelation. However, in his commentary on "No compulsion is there in religion," al-Razi begins with the explanation based on Mu'tazilite theology which maintains that God has made the faith abundantly clear to the human intellect and thus there remains no excuse for human beings to reject it. But if they do so, it is because they are free agents and accountable for their deeds. Nevertheless, no authority can compel human beings to believe. This is corroborated by 10:99, which says: "If thy Lord had willed, whoever is in the earth would have believed, all of them, all together. Wouldst thou [O Muhammad] then constrain the people, until they are believers?" Al-Razi does not offer any criticism of this Mu'tazili view, which tends to show that he tacitly approved this rationalist interpretation, so explicit in the Qur'an (*Tafsir*, 7/15).

17. al-Tabari, *Tafsir*, 3/10-12; al-Razi, *Tafsir*, 4/15-16. In a recent work, *The Jews of Islam* (Princeton: Princeton University Press, 1984), Bernard Lewis, a prominent Orientalist, has treated the question of tolerance, in the sense of "acceptance by a dominant religion of the presence of others," in Islam. He has limited his inquiry to the record of Muslim history—a record of the way Islam in power treated other religions. In other words, Lewis's inquiry deals with the historical treatment of religious minorities by the upholders of Muslim authority and law. However, in the process of showing that in Islam intolerance in the sense that "discrimination was always there, permanent and indeed necessary, inherent in the system and institutionalized in law and practice," (p. 8), Lewis has neglected to take into account the overall Qur'anic stance on the acceptance of religious pluralism, and thus failed to give an adequate evaluation of the ideal factors in Islam that support religious liberty. Thus, for example, the verse "No compulsion is there in religion" has been regarded by Lewis (on the basis of a recent study by an European scholar and against all the exegetical literature on the Qur'an) as being "not a commendation of tolerance but rather an expression of resignation—an almost reluctant acceptance of the obduracy of others," (p. 13). Such an interpretation of the "No compulsion" verse must be weighed against the overwhelming concern of the Qur'an to make it amply clear that not only is the existence of diversity of religions an accepted divine mystery; it is also supposed to generate awareness among the religious communities, including the Muslim community, that they should avoid exclusivist claims. Lewis's inadequate account indicates even more the importance of studying the Qur'anic references dealing with the question of tolerance or intolerance toward Jews or other minorities in the light of the religion-morality distinction that we have argued for in this discussion of the Qur'an.

18. al-Zamakhshari, *Kashaf*, 1/387.

19. David Little, "Duties of Station vs. Duties of Conscience: Are There Two Moralities?" *Private and Public Ethics: Tensions Between Conscience and Institutional Responsibility*, ed. Donald G. Jones (New York: Edwin Mellen Press, 1978), 136.

20. C. D. Broad, "Conscience and Conscientious Action," *Conscience*, ed. Donnelly and Lyons (New York: Alba House, 1973), 8.

21. Muhammad 'Abduh, *al-Manar*, 1/62–65.

22. Rahman, *Major Themes*, 44.

23. In his recent article, "Religious Liberty: A Muslim Perspective," Muhammad Talbi has pointed to the problem with the Muslim jurists of the Classical Age who had failed to see the Qur'anic references to apostasy in a religio-moral perspective. More to the point is Hamid Enayat's observation regarding the implications of Ali'Abd al-Raziq's work on the caliphate and the question of the self-subsistence of moral values. According to Enayat, "The crux of any exaltation of the Prophet's spiritual, as opposed to his political or military leadership is that it is

also an exaltation of individual conscience versus forcible, collective conformism. This is not a vision alien to Islam—witness all those Qur'anic verses absolving the Prophet from responsibility for the salvation of individual Muslims, something which is essentially the fruit of their own actions. The systematized form of this vision is moral philosophy which values good deeds only in so far as they are anchored in the fulfilled conscience of their agents and not in the fear of any external sanctions, immediate or eschatological." (*Modern Islamic Political Thought* [Austin: University Texas Press, 1982], 68).

24. For unlawful intercourse: "The fornicatress and the fornicator, scourge each one of them a hundred stripes" (24:2); false accusation: "And those who (accuse honorable women) and then bring not four witnesses, scourge them with eighty stripes" (24:2); theft: "And the thief, male and female: cut off the hands of both" (5:38); and highway robbery: "This is the recompense of those who (make war upon) God and His Messenger, and (strive after corruption in the land:) they shall be slaughtered, or crucified" (5:33). The last citation is also used to justify capital punishment for rebellion.

25. Theoretically, *ta'zir* crimes are those that bring injury to the social order as a result of the trouble they cause, and it was for this reason that their precise punishment was left to the community and its representatives, the caliphs. See Ahman 'Abd al-Aziz al-Alfi, "Punishment in the Islamic Criminal Law," *The Islamic Criminal Justice System,* ed. M. Cherif Bassiouni (New York: Oceana, 1982), 227; also S. M. Zwemer, *The Law of Apostasy in Islam* (London, 1924), esp. cha. 2. This latter work, although outdated and hostile in some places, is still useful as a summary of laws of apostasy in Islam.

26. *Sunan Abi Dawud,* 4/126. See also the study on the sources of penal law by Taymour Kamil, "The Principle of Legality and Its Application in Islamic Criminal Justice," *The Islamic Criminal Justice System,* 149-69.

27. Joseph Schacht, *Introduction to Islamic Law* (Oxford, 1976), 176.

28. al-Tabari, *Ta'rikh al-rusul wa al-muluk* (Cairo, 1962), 3/249-52, mentions the letters of Abu Bakr to the defecting tribes. He then proceeds to describe in a long section (pp. 253-342) all the other tribes in different parts of Arabia who had regarded their agreement with Muhammad as canceled after the Prophet's death.

29. al-Tabari, *Tafsir* 5/124-5; al-Zamakhshari, *Kashshaf* 1/550; Baydawi, *Anwar,* 121.

30. al-Tabari, *Tafsir,* 6/133; al-Zamakhshari, *Kashshaf* 1/609; Baydawi, *Anwar,* 145.

31. Fazlur Rahman, in the introduction to his *Islam and Modernity: Transformation of an Intellectual Tradition* (Chicago: University of Chicago Press, 1982), points out the lack of method and hermeneutics among the Muslim scholars who were engaged in deducing law from the Qur'an. The reason for this lack, according to Rahman, was that the intellectual instrument for deriving law and other social institutions (such as analogical reasoning) lacked the capacity, to the requisite degree, for making legal derivations. This imperfection of the intellectual instrument was in turn due to the lack of an adequate method for understanding the Qur'an itself.

32. Rahman, *Major Themes,* 63; also 159-60, where he discusses the justification for *jihad* in the sense of "strong-willed resistance to the pressure of *fitna* [a situation where a person is pressured by others to defect from his affiliations or retreat from his views, especially by close relatives] and retaliation in case of violence." Rahman sees *jihad,* at least in the context of Medina, as "an organized and total effort of the community—if necessary through war—to overcome the hurdles in the way of the spread of Islam." Such a purpose for *jihad* could not contradict what has been said in connection with the enforcement of the standard of justice by the state, if by the spread of Islam is meant the protection of the political domain of Islam, without encroaching upon the basic freedom of religion.

CONCLUSION

In the Introduction to this study we stated that discussion relative to human rights is still at an early stage compared to other fields of inquiry. Our hope was to contribute to the advance of human rights discussion by developing a set of essays in comparative religious ethics, framed in terms of human rights issues. In particular, we wished to address the question of how Islam, as a religious tradition distinct from Western Christianity, relates to the ideas of religious liberty and freedom of conscience that are so important both in the West and in the international discussion of human rights.

Obviously we think that comparative studies of religious traditions have an important place in discussions of human rights. We hope that our study has opened the way for other related efforts. However, it does not seem out of place to emphasize that there is more room for dialogue between Islam and the West on matters of religious liberty than (it seems) has been thought, both by Westerners and Muslims. In particular, given the incidence of Islamic disagreement with respect to Article 18 of the Universal Declaration of Human Rights (Kelsay), a disagreement that appears to have been brought about in part by differing ways of approaching and appropriating the message of the Qur'an, we have been led to scrutinize the Qur'anic message in terms of freedom of conscience and religion (Sachedina). The result of this scrutiny, informed throughout by the comments of exegetes traditionally regarded in Muslim circles as authoritative or at least significant, is the suggestion that the Qur'an posits, or contains evidence for, a kind of universal guidance which, in its availability to all humanity seems parallel to the Western-Christian idea of a natural moral law. Similarly, careful study of the Qur'an seems to indicate that several notions (particularly *fitra* and *qalb*) combine to suggest a personal capacity to know and act on the good that is analogous to the Western-Christian conscience.

Most importantly, and perhaps most controversially, it appears that the Qur'anic emphasis upon this personal capacity to know and act, coupled with the ultimate purpose of universal guidance—which is the leading of human beings to the acknowledgment of God as their Lord—implies the personal, inward nature of faith, or of the choosing of faith, which in the hands of some Christian theologians has produced the doctrine of religious liberty. This idea, made explicit in such Qur'anic verses as "There is no compulsion in religion" (2:256), would seem to be at the heart of Qur'anic teaching on the relation between God and humanity. It would also seem to have important implications for any Islamic polity; it certainly suggests a number of possibilities for the discussion of human rights in relation to the cultures of the West and Islam.

The controversial aspect of this point is, as Sachedina's essay makes clear, its variance from much of traditional Islamic teaching, particularly as it is formulated in the legal schools. Such teaching, which suggests very harsh penalties for certain types of apostasy, is in opposition to the interpretation of the Qur'an which he advocates. This is so, he suggests, because of a certain confusion about the role of an Islamic government as the means by which the Qur'anic demand for a just public order is to be fulfilled, as well as a certain gray area in the relation between religious and moral duties in an Islamic system. The government envisioned by the Qur'an need not, apparently, punish apostasy as a crime against God, since its role in the struggle for justice is fulfilled through the enforcement of that universal guidance which is the presupposition for individual conscience. And indeed, such a government may exceed its bounds, since the Qur'an explicitly assigns the right of judgment in matters of faith to God, the Lord of the Worlds. There is, however, a sense in which apostasy, as an undercutting through denial of the revealed guidance which God provides in the Qur'an, may be a "spreading of corruption" and thus a threat to public order, to be punished by the state.

Thus, Sachedina's discussion of the Qur'an may be taken to indicate certain possibilities for Western-Islamic exchanges on religious liberty. In response to the question which Kelsay raises, pertaining to the Islamic status of Zafrullah Khan's statements at the United Nations, it seems there *is* a basis for religious liberty in the Qur'an, and that modernist tendencies in this regard cannot be taken simply as the result of Western influence. Similarly, in response to Little's exposition of the themes in Christian thought making for a society organized to allow for and protect religious liberty, and his suggestion that similar themes run deep in the scripture of Islam, it seems possible to affirm that the Qur'an, as understood by Muslim commentators, contains elements which support a religiously pluralistic, even liberal society.

There are also problems for religious liberty in an Islamic context. Following Sachedina's account, we can begin to locate these in terms of a demand for the creation and sustenance of a just public order. As he has argued, it is certainly possible, and perhaps closer to the spirit of the Qur'anic message, to understand this demand as pertaining to and fulfilled by an enforcement of universal guidance, apart from the establishment of any particular religious provisions. On the other hand, the conceptual confusion he attributes to the schools of law and the gray area involving the use of force against those who spread corruption suggest a difficult tension which, one might say, seems to be expressed in the disagreement between representatives of Islamic states— for example, Saudi Arabia and Pakistan—on questions of religious liberty. Given the possibility of conflicting assessments of the Qur'anic provisions for freedom of religion in relation to its demand for public order, it is difficult to know what, precisely, is *the* Islamic position on matters pertaining to religious liberty—that is, to know with precision what the relation of Islam, as a religious tradition shaping lives and patterns of culture around the world, is to the "international form of discourse" suggested by human rights agreements and their advocates. There are, it seems, ways of approaching the Qur'anic message which allow for Ash'arites and Mu'tazilites (in the Classical Period) or for Wahhabis and modernists (more recently) to claim for themselves the status of people "responding to the Qur'an." If we are to avoid turning too simply or too quickly to the positions of these, or other sectors of the Islamic community, as representing true Islam, what are we to do? At the very least, those interested in a dialogic approach to questions of human rights in relation to Islam should begin to be more sensitive to the diversity within this formidable tradition.

At the same time, as Little's essay shows, it is no simple matter to say with precision what *the* Christian position is as regards religious liberty. Thus, while there seem to be clear and important affinities between the thought of a Roger Williams, for example, and the institutionalization of religious liberty which Western culture seems to take for granted, it is not (or at least has not always been) so plain that Christian theology is supportive of such an arrangement. Little's essay indicates that ideas of conscience and natural law have played an important part in Christian thinking since New Testament times; but he also indicates there have been various appropriations of these

Conclusion

ideas by Christian thinkers reflecting on the social arrangements of their time. Thus, Thomas Aquinas or John Calvin or John Cotton could hold finally to a very different vision of the just society from Roger Williams, particularly on the treatment of apostates or dissenters—groups whose treatment constitutes a kind of test case for ideas of religious liberty. Again, if we are to avoid identifying too quickly one or another sector of the Christian community as *the* holder of Christian truth, or if we are to avoid simple acceptance of current social arrangements as' the measure of Christian thought, we shall have to take this diversity seriously. And thus Christianity presents us with problems as well as possibilities for human rights discussion no less, it seems, than does Islam.

These points present us with, to recall our earlier phrase, "staggeringly large questions." The importance of comparative inquiry notwithstanding, it is exceedingly difficult to know what *the* relationship of Islam or of Christianity to formulations of human rights might be. Accordingly, one conclusion of our study might be to reiterate the early argument of Kelsay's chapter, that a dialogic approach to comparative studies requires attention to the various statements of representatives of Islamic (or Western) culture on the matters at hand (here, religious liberty). In addition, one wants to avoid identifying Islam (or Christianity) with one or a few of the particular representations of that tradition. We must listen, but not uncritically. If we ask about the relation of Islam to human rights, we are likely to be told many things. The job of the comparativist is to sort out these claims, to understand the differing arguments of various adherents inside the respective traditions, and, in the model which Little develops, to examine these claims as possibilities implicit in the "lineage of ideas" present in such traditions.

To leave it at that, however, would be to ignore the direction in which our study has led us—one that we think is important to state, even though it is controversial. If our first conclusion, tied to the recognition of diversity within the religious traditions we are here interested in, leads to a recommendation about the care necessary in comparative and descriptive work, our second conclusion leads in a normative direction. While it is true that the lineage of ideas in both Christianity and Islam is diverse, it also seems true that the "logic" of each faith pushes toward a recognition of religious liberty as an important corollary to the notion of true belief. It is, of course, historically true that most societies informed by these two religious traditions have not organized themselves in terms of the protection of religious liberty. In that sense both Islam and Christianity have, more often than not, given rise to the kind of social organization associated with religious toleration—that is, to a kind of pluralism under the umbrella of a state religion which, while hardly equivalent to tyranny, is far from the religious liberty advocated in contemporary human rights formulations. It is this kind of arrangement which appears to be envisioned by the law schools of Islam, on the one hand, and by Christian theologians such as Aquinas, Calvin, and Cotton, on the other. And where religiously liberal arrangements have been advocated, as (apparently) in Pakistani modernism or in the thought of Roger Williams, their advocates have proceeded, of necessity, through the use of a kind of "Protestant principle," by which existing ideas and arrangements have been criticized on the basis of a return to, or reinterpretation of, original sources (the Qur'an or the Bible).

Such a return or reinterpretation does not settle all problems, of course. We have seen that, to a certain extent, disagreement in the Islamic and Christian communities may be attributed to the variety of interpretive possibilities the basic texts present. Our suggestion, however, on the basis of our studies of Islam and Christianity, is that these texts present a picture of true belief, tied to the workings of conscience and natural law, which pushes toward the idea of religious liberty and its accompanying social arrangements. Given the argument presented in Little's essay—that the very notion of religion or religious belief seems to imply an authority and a realm of action which is beyond the (proper) control of human beings—that would seem to be expected. Christianity and Islam are nothing if not *religious* traditions, in this sense: that the workings of a sacred authority which is to an important degree beyond human control and which in effect is an appropriate determining factor in human affairs, are part and parcel of their views of reality. That this sacred authority would exercise a special authority in the realm of faith and religious practice that is above and outside human civil control seems logically to follow.

This does not mean, of course, that tensions between religious and moral perspectives, or between spiritual and temporal realms, or inner and outer workings of human beings, do not or will not exist. As has been shown, there are various ways in which both Islamic and Christian thought have dealt with these, which from the perspective of this study are distinctions implicit in the notion of religion. As Little puts it, various traditions (or various appropriations of diverse traditions) may draw the lines between these at different points.

Perhaps the most important thing to recognize is that the distinctions *are made* in different traditions; that Islam and Christianity *do* recognize the existence of these points around which the relationship of religious belief and social organization take shape. Our particular account about the ways in which Christianity and Islam do, or should, draw the lines between religious and moral responsibility, or between those inner workings of the spirit which are God's affair and that external behavior which it is the interest of the state to regulate, may be evaluated apart from this. For if it be granted that the questions asked by Islamic and Christian traditions are similar, a dialogic approach such as we have attempted has much to offer, and we can continue to talk about the values articulated in discussions of human rights in the hope that these discussions can generate deeper mutual understanding across cultural barriers, and more fervent common commitment to the universal cause of human rights.

APPENDIX 1

Al-Bukhari's Hadith on "Killing Those Who Refuse to Fulfill the Duties Enjoined by God and Considering Them Apostates"

In chapter 3 of this volume I mentioned that the Arab tribes had demanded remission of the *zakat* tax—a demand which Abu Bakr rejected indignantly. The bloody battle that ensued was in order to suppress their revolt against the Medina government. Thus, at the center of the issue was the refusal to pay the divinely ordained *zakat* tax, which the nascent Islamic government was demanding by virtue of the authority invested in it as the representative of the Muslim community. It is relevant to point out that the *zakat* tax, which was levied on certain designated types of property, could not (at least in this early period) have been strictly regarded as alms to be distributed among the poor members of the community, since it was used for military enterprises and other political purposes. Accordingly, *zakat* provided revenues used in such a way that the tax could serve both religious and moral purposes and could be construed as a religious obligation as well as a moral duty. At one level, among the religiously inclined, the giving away of worldly possessions in the form of *zakat* was regarded as a pious act ordained by God; at another level it fulfilled a moral obligation pertaining to the welfare of the members of the Muslim community.[1] Indeed, in its Qur'anic usage the term *zakat* denotes virtue and righteousness in general, and the Qur'an lays stress on the practice of *zakat* in this sense, declaring it to be one of the chief virtues of the true believer (e.g. 13:22, 35:29).

The Arab tribes who adopted Islam during the Prophet's time had to pay the *zakat*, the amount of which was usually fixed in the agreements made with the Prophet. It is plausible to maintain, on the basis of early sources, that the character of *zakat* in the time of the Prophet was vague; it represented more a tax demanded by the representative of the Medina polity than Islamic religion. In other words, the tribes understood it as a purely political, not religious, tax. It was for this reason that after the Prophet's death many Arab tribes refused to continue to pay *zakat*, as they considered that their agreement with the Medina government had been canceled with the death of the Prophet. On the other hand, Abu Bakr in his communications to these tribes emphasized the point that they had to fulfill what they had once promised (payment of *zakat*) because their agreement was not with Muhammad, the mortal being, but with God, whom Muhammad represented as his messenger, Abu Bakr being the successor to Muhammad as the leader of Medina. That Abu Bakr was approaching the problem of the rebelling Arab tribes from this particular stance is well demonstrated by al-Bukhari's tradition (*hadith*) relating the caliph's controversy with 'Umar (d. 644), who eventually succeeded him, concerning the justification for killing those Arab tribesmen who refused to pay the *zakat* tax.

The importance of this tradition cannot be overstressed, because it has been cited as documentation by all Muslim jurists when dealing with the legality of fighting tyrants and apostates. Accordingly, its soundness has not been questioned by any scholar. Let us cite the tradition which appears in a section entitled "Killing those who refuse to fulfill the duties enjoined by God and considering them apostates." The *hadith* reads as follows:

> It is narrated by Abu Hurayra that when the Prophet died and Abu Bakr became his successor and some of the Arabs reverted to disbelief, 'Umar said: "O Abu Bakr! How can you fight these people in spite of what the Messenger of God has said, 'I have been commanded to fight the people till they say: There is no god but God. And whoever declared: There is no god but God, God will save his property and his life from me, unless [that person commits an act for which he deserved legal penalty] justly, and his reckoning will be with God.' "
>
> Abu Bakr said: "I solemnly declare that I will fight whoever differentiates between prayer and *zakat*, as *zakat* is the right to be taken from property. By God! if they refused to pay me even an ewe lamb they used to pay to God's Messenger, I would fight them for withholding it."
>
> 'Umar said: "By God! It was nothing, but I noticed that God opened Abu Bakr's chest towards the decision to fight. Therefore, I realized that his decision was right."[2]

The tradition shows the existence of a difference of opinion and a tension experienced by Muslim leaders in dealing with the matter of *zakat*, which actually symbolized the politicoreligious agreement between the Prophet and the tribes. 'Umar, according to this tradition, was inclined to agree with the Arab tribes who apparently had not abandoned the basic tenet of Islamic faith, namely the belief in the unity of God. This is implied in 'Umar's argument concerning their guaranteed security as long as they acknowledged the unity of God. Moreover, 'Umar separates *zakat* from the declaration of faith, explicitly indicating that *zakat* was part of an agreement between the Prophet and the tribes which was canceled by the Prophet's death.

Accordingly 'Umar, as his statement indicates, felt the demand for the remission of *zakat* after the Prophet's death did not constitute a violation against God or his messenger for which severe penalties could be invoked in accordance with the Qur'anic injunction. In other words, 'Umar seems to be making the point that the tribes did not turn from their basic religious belief and consequently did not pose a threat to the legitimacy of the Medina polity. On the other hand, Abu Bakr, who saw Islamic public order having not a limited but a total jurisdiction over the life of the community under its authority, regarded the demand of the tribes as constituting not only an act of disobedience to God and his Prophet but also a challenge to the authority which, by virtue of its being acknowledged as successor to the Prophet, had the right to enforce the terms of contract the tribes had once accepted. Thus, in Abu Bakr's treatment of the tribes we have a clear instance of a political violation being punished as a violation against Islam as a politicoreligious system, without any attempt at separating the two entities. Interestingly, Abu Bakr's refusal to separate the prayer (declaration of faith) and the *zakat* seems to be making a point Thomas Aquinas makes in the Christian context when he justifies the use of force against heretics and apostates because they failed "to carry out what they promised and to hold what they once accepted."

It is important to bear in mind that the Bukhari version of the Abu Bakr-'Umar controversy regarding the treatment of the rebelling tribes seems to have been edited by the narrator, the tendency being, as time passed, to idealize such early personages as Abu Bakr and 'Umar. In this case the two figures were made to appear in full agreement with each other. That aside, it is evident that the tradition in and of itself does not deal with a case of apostasy in the sense of "turning back from religion" because the tribesmen, according to 'Umar's argument, had not turned from their basic religious belief; rather, it was a case of rebellion against the Islamic polity. And thus Abu Bakr was determined to resolve the problem in accordance with the sanction provided by the Qur'an for this kind of violation (5:33–34).

What was involved in this case, then, was a conflict of understanding between the Arab tribes and Abu Bakr over the basis of the Arabs' obligation

Appendix 1

to pay *zakat*. The Arabs believed their responsibility to pay the tax was terminated upon the death of the Prophet, while Abu Bakr contended that the Arabs' obligation to pay the tax was part of their continuing commitment to Islam. Their resistance constituted a threat to the stability and viability of the established political order. This was, therefore, not perceived as a question of apostasy at all, but of the obligations of membership in the Islamic community.

NOTES

1. For similar discussion pertaining to the complexity of religious-moral distinction in the Gospel of Matthew, see David Little and Sumner B. Twiss, *Comparative Religious Ethics: A New Method* (1978), where the authors have maintained the necessity and possibility of rigorous distinction of moral and religious categories.

2. *Sahih al-Bukhari, Bab al-murtaddun, hadith* #59.

Appendix 2

United Nations Resolution on the Elimination of Intolerance Based on Religion

Resolution Adopted by the General Assembly [on the Report of the Third Committee (A/36/684)] 36/55. *Declaration on the Elimination of All Forms of Intolerance and of Discrimination Based on Religion or Belief*

Considering that one of the basic principles of the Charter of the United Nations is that of the dignity and equality inherent in all human beings, and that all Member States have pledged themselves to take joint and separate action in co-operation with the Organization to promote and encourage universal respect for the observance of human rights and fundamental freedoms for all, without distinction as to race, sex, language or religion,

Considering that the Universal Declaration on Human Rights [General Assembly Resolution 217A (III)] and the International Covenants on Human Rights [General Assembly Resolution 2200A (XXI)] proclaim the principles of non-discrimination and equality before the law and the right to freedom of thought, conscience, religion and belief,

Considering that the disregard and infringement of human rights and fundamental freedoms, in particular of the right to freedom of thought, conscience, religion or whatever belief, have brought, directly or indirectly, wars and great suffering to mankind, especially where they serve as a means of foreign interference in the internal affairs of other States and amount to kindling hatred between peoples and nations,

Considering that religion or belief, for anyone who professes either, is one of the fundamental elements in his conception of life and that freedom of religion or belief should be fully respected and guaranteed,

Considering that it is essential to promote understanding, tolerance and respect in matters relating to freedom of religion and belief and to ensure that the use of religion or belief for ends inconsistent with the Charter, other relevant instruments of the United Nations and the purposes and principles of the present Declaration is inadmissable,

Convinced that freedom of religion and belief should also contribute to the attainment of the goals of world peace, social justice and friendship among peoples and to the elimination of ideologies or practices of colonialism and racial discrimination,

Noting with satisfaction the adoption of several, and the coming force of some, conventions, under the aegis of the United Nations and of the specialized agencies, for the elimination of various forms of discrimination,

Concerned by manifestations of intolerance and by the existence of discrimination in matters of religion or belief still in evidence in some areas of the world,

Resolved to adopt all necessary measures for the speedy elimination of such intolerance in all its forms and manifestations and to prevent and combat discrimination on the grounds of religion of belief,

Proclaims this Declaration on the Elimination of All Forms of Intolerance and of Discrimination Based on Religion or Belief:

Article 1

1. Everyone shall have the right to freedom of thought, conscience and religion. This right shall include freedom to have a religion or whatever belief of his choice, and freedom, either individually or in community with others, and in public or private, to manifest his religion or belief in worship, observance, practice and teaching.

2. No one shall be subject to coercion which would impair his freedom to have a religion or belief of his choice.

3. Freedom to manifest one's religion or beliefs may be subject only to such limitations as are prescribed by law and are necessary to protect public

safety, order, health or morals or the fundamental rights and freedoms of others.

Article 2

1. No one shall be subject to discrimination by any State, institution, group of persons or person on the grounds of religion or other beliefs.

2. For the purposes of the present Declaration, the expression "intolerance and discrimination based on religion or belief" means any distinction, exclusion, restriction or preference based on religion or belief and having as its purpose or as its effect nullification or impairment of the recognition, enjoyment or exercise of human rights and fundamental freedoms on an equal basis.

Article 3

Discrimination between human beings on the grounds of religion or belief constitutes an affront to human dignity and a disavowal of the principles of the Charter of the United Nations, and shall be condemned as a violation of the human rights and fundamental freedoms proclaimed in the Universal Declaration on Human Rights and enunciated in detail in the International Covenants on Human Rights, and as an obstacle to friendly and peaceful relations between nations.

Article 4

1. All States shall take effective measures to prevent and eliminate discrimination on the grounds of religion or belief in the recognition, exercise and enjoyment of human rights and fundamental freedoms in all fields of civil, economic, political, social and cultural life.

2. All States shall make all efforts to enact or rescind legislation where necessary to prohibit any such discrimination, and to take all appropriate measures to combat intolerance on the grounds of religion or other beliefs in this matter.

Article 5

1. The parents or, as the case may be, the legal guardians of the child have the right to organize the life within the family in accordance with their religion or belief and bearing in mind the moral education in which they believe the child should be brought up.

2. Every child shall enjoy the right to have access to education in the

matter of religion or belief in accordance with the wishes of his parents or legal guardians, the best interests of the child being the guiding principle.

3. The child shall be protected from any form of discrimination on the grounds of religion or belief. He shall be brought up in a spirit of understanding, tolerance, friendship among peoples, peace and universal brotherhood, respect for freedom of religion or belief of others, and in full consciousness that his energy and talents should be devoted to the service of his fellow men.

4. In the case of a child who is not under the care either of his parents or of legal guardians, due account shall be taken of their expressed wishes or of any other proof of their wishes in the matter of religion or belief, the best interests of the child being the guiding principle.

5. Practices of a religion or beliefs in which a child is brought up must not be injurious to his physical or mental health or to his full development, taking into account article 1, paragraph 3, of the present Declaration.

Article 6

In accordance with article 1 of the present Declaration, and subject to the provisions of article 1, paragraph 3, the right to freedom of thought, conscience, religion or belief shall include, *inter alia,* the following freedoms:

(a) To worship or assemble in connexion with a religion or belief, and to establish and maintain places for these purposes;

(b) To establish and maintain appropriate charitable or humanitarian institutions;

(c) To make, acquire and use to an adequate extent the necessary articles and materials related to the rites or customs of a religion or belief;

(d) To write, issue and disseminate relevant publications in these areas;

(e) To teach a religion or belief in places suitable for these purposes;

(f) To solicit and receive voluntary financial and other contributions from individuals and institutions;

(g) To train, appoint, elect or designate by succession appropriate leaders called for by the requirements and standards of any religion or belief;

(h) To observe days of rest and to celebrate holidays and ceremonies in accordance with the precepts of one's religion or belief;

(i) To establish and maintain communications with individuals and communities in matters of religion and belief at the national and international levels.

Article 7

The rights and freedoms set forth in the present Declaration shall be accorded in national legislations in such a manner that everyone shall be able to avail himself of such rights and freedoms in practice.

Article 8

Nothing in the present Declaration shall be construed as restricting or derogating from any right defined in the Universal Declaration on Human Rights and the International Covenants on Human Rights.

73rd plenary meeting
25 November 1981

Index

107

Scriptural Citations

Qur'an

1:4	75	6:113	29
1:5	73	6:125	59
2:2	58, 59	6:153	63
2:5	58	6:160	29, 73
2:10	60	8:49	69
2:26	60	9	30
2:73	60	9:13	84, 85
2:74	70	9:29	7
2:112	64	9:38	75
2:117	30, 63	9:41	84
2:180	62	9:71	76
2:213	61, 74	10:99	29, 66, 68, 76
2:216	30, 67	10:100	66
2:217	30	11:118	74
2:218	30	13:22	97
2:255	80	13:28	70
2:256	29, 66, 67, 92	16:9	73
2:257	72	18:6	67
3:8	60	18:57	69
3:19	73	19:104	59
3:90	60	20:2	67
3:104	76	30:129	65, 66
3:110	76	35:29	97
4:33	85	49:14	66
4:61	63	50:37	70
4:70	59	50:45	76
4:88	81	61:5	60–61
4:89	6, 30, 81	67:25	6
4:91	84	69:19	29
4:128	63	70:19	58
5:33	6, 77, 82, 99	70:20	58
5:34	77, 99	79:35	71
5:48	64, 75	91:7	58, 61, 65
6:107	75	91:8	58, 64, 65, 71
6:108	29, 75	91:9	58, 65
6:109	75	91:10	58, 65
6:110	75	109	29
6:111	75		

Bible

1 Corinthians 8:7	14
2 Corinthians 2:12	14
Romans 2:14	14, 62
Romans 2:15	14, 62
Romans 3:19	14, 62